From a student to a pro leadership guide

THE

DEGREE

Of

PERCEPTION

Towards business
& LEADERSHIP

TATENDA D NDURU

Catalogue-in-Publication Data for this book is
available in the National Archives of Zimbabwe,
National Library and Documentation Services.

ISBN 978-1-7792-1408-9

EAN 9781779214089

DEDICATION

This book is dedicated to my beautiful mom for being supportive and believing in my dreams. Also, people who have shared knowledge related to business, psychology, spirituality, finance, and leadership through books, audios, videos etc. I tried to recall everything that changed my psychology into that of a leader.

"I believe each and everyone can be a leader and it all starts within."

CONTENTS

Light Before Reading

In this book, the use of **He** is not representing/supporting any gender, but rather make explanations clear for any he/she.

The author will review human-animal resemblance during an individual's growth from limited perceptions to unlimited perceptions in business and leadership.

This book will help in understanding what it takes to be in the underlined degree while giving setbacks in each psychology, and knowledge on how to grow for the next chapter.

He will be looking at the spiritual, educational, financial, (+relationship) perceptions to support the core of each individual's psychology.

P.s, the hedgehog approach was created for growth, mastery and educational purposes…not to entertain.

CHAPTER 1

THE SHEEP: The Tongue Of The Wise Commends Knowledge, But The Mouth Of The Fool Gushes Folly...(Proverbs 15:2)

The follower

This is a group of people whose skills are hidden by undisciplined and or dependent behaviours, like the way they think, talk, and live.

Psychology of the sheep

Have you ever encounter people who think they do not deserve anything good in life? Beings who unconsciously submitted to the fact that they are poor, or think they don't deserve a happy ever after relationship, or a different life story after they have failed or commit a mistake?. In this mindset, a being believes that he has never done anything worthwhile to make something good come true, and when he sees good things, and opportunities, he already subtracts himself since he perceives that 'there are other people who were made better than others in terms of talents and knowledge. And within this perception, a being is afraid to start anything because the thought of failure paralyses the mind, so he prefers to stay how he was before than trying to do something which he does not know how it will be or end.

This psychology runs an individual life to the extent of switching off the drive to prepare for anything uncertain in the future since he does not have any clue about what to prepare for. And when you ask them why are you not even trying to improve yourself, they say things like "life is too short, we gonna die anyway" or "life has no formula and is too complicated" or "what if it doesn't work" or "I will not get anything either way" or "I will fail anyway".

In sheep psychology, preparation is a waste of time since he does not know the results of his actions. He views life as very complicated, thinking that life will only bring unpredictable outcomes.

Though he believes that other people know how to predict future outcomes and possess talent, however, he just thinks that it is not him who can do it in his life and in any situation which he perceives to lack the talent.

This develops his psychology to believe that his abilities cannot be changed and are fixed, as stated on a being with a fixed mindset who believes that "one's ability is mostly innate and cannot be changed", by (Dweck 2017).

This belief makes a being follow other individuals perceiving them to help him to flourish or give support, believing he can not do what he wants alone.

In this perception, a being also believes that everything should be free regardless of how much effort and processes were taken to provide what's at hand. This leads to demand free things like free education, free housing, free services, and even free money from other people. In mind, he does not even consider or thinks about the struggle and or other human efforts which need to be appreciated that have made something come true.

When facing a situation which he does not perceive value or not afford, you will hear him saying "life is not fair", or "these guys stole from me", or "this was too much for me", or "l didn't want it to be this way", causing him to perceive that for everything to be fair it should be handed to him.

This psychology weakens personal beliefs as one becomes vulnerable to complaints when the real world ends up not presenting those wishes.

Spiritual Perceptions

Prayer with no work

(Proverbs 10:4)"Lazy hands make a man poor, but diligent hands bring wealth"

In this perception, an individual understands the importance of praying as the only weapon towards his success. He prays very hard to the extend of prayer paralysis- 'a state where an individual resolves all his problems in a prayer to make up excuses of not working for what he just prayed for'.

In this state a being feels that the efforts which he has put in the prayer will work in his life in form of miracles, so he uses God as an excuse to avoid work and develop apathy and laziness, this leads him to go back on his normal routine after the prayer to wait for the miracle while doing nothing. What happens next? Nothing happens! he becomes poorer and his children inheriting poverty.

And at the end of the day you will hear him saying there is no God, if he is there, why is he not replying? But speaking fact he is replying in a way you should understand.

So for a being to grow from this perception, he should understand that "God installed all the replies and required capabilities in an individual with extra guidance around people, He(God) only requires a being to work towards a certain goal around the purpose which he was created for".

To keep growing from this perception an individual should

continue to "pray as if no work would help, but should also work as if no prayer would help him".

When a being knows the impact of working on his prayer, he will stop relying on God and other people to do the work which he is supposed to do. He will grow to become a being who prays hard and work hard, and if he works to find out that he has reached his limitations, he should pray unto his God for help to proceed from where he has left off.

One religion close to God than the other?

In this perception, an individual believes that his religion is the only way to God, and desires to destroy other beliefs which contrasts with how he understands the supernatural world. He perceives that God is inactive amid all other religions outside his own beliefs and culture, yet for a fact, God is active in every religion and culture. Every religion that believes to be the existence of Creator God and view him as the father who is always there for his children who never abandon them, and always protect his children from enemies is true religion. A religion with the creator God who invites every human being in that particular religion to seek him while on the other hand, him as God seeking with persistence for human beings to give them his grace.

In this perception, we have monotheists who believe in the existence of one God, the God of Noah the Semite.

This is the background since everyone that is existing now after the time of Noah, comes from the Semite who took animals and his family into the ark and must have come from that family. However, human beings do believe in different religions due to their cultures but the background of defining God is the same from Christianity, Islam, Judaism, Buddhism to African Tradition.

And these religions have been gradually existing over the years because it is God's will to keep these religions alive. He wants to keep all these religions alive because he is the universal God who is above every human religion, culture, and language.

The understanding of each different individual's conception of God in other religions or the same religion and cultures, - requires a being to grow by learning other forms of expressions and understandings from those other individuals. This helps a being to measure the behaviour triggered by those individual beliefs and come to choose how to connect with others, - and more with the Creator God in harmony.

Somehow these perceptions about one religion which is close to God than others have been influenced by religious leaders. Religious leaders who manipulate the one God code of conduct to their own will by creating perceptions that suit their earthly desires and teach their followers a polluted word that separates mankind by disturbing peace and harmony.

This manipulation of religious conduct finds its way to lead followers to forget that, 'the existence of spirituality is to keep a being in the path of positive mysticism while supporting peace and harmony with other living creatures '.

This manipulation also creates psychology around the followers to destroy this purpose by declaring enmity with other individuals who approach God in ways which one was not taught around a well-developed religion.

This psychology develops individuals who are not eager to learn and weigh how other people contact the universal God which might help to improve from limited views.

So for a being to keep growing from this perception he should know that the growth of a being in the future is not about if he is a believer or not, but the growth of one's knowledge and education to understand more of the universal God towards supporting peace and harmony in the world.

Fixed ways to a prayer?

Many individuals grew to learn to understand their religion from the preceding generation on how to communicate with God based on how effective their types of prayers were in the past.

The elder people then teach young individuals how to practise these forms of prayers and other ways to communicate with the creator God. This then groomed their next generation to follow the doctrine of that preceding generation by numbering certain rules and practises which are expected by God for well-being.

This set of practices teach a being to know what's right and what's wrong in the world, also growing them into beings who are directed to live their life morally which pleases the creator God. This developed their traditional ways of praying and other communications to reach God, as it has been done by their former religious leaders who were shown the path by God through a certain type of successful prayer.

As their creator God answered, they came to create communications, developing religious cultures and beliefs around that background.

However, many individuals depending on their religions grew to believe that the ways which they were taught are the only ways to communicate with the creator God. They grew to believe that their type of God-related communications are the right ones and might be the only way to reach out to the creator God. Then as they collide with other individuals who believe their different doctrine, the sheep perception manifests in form of judgements on the other beings,- judging how wrong they are to the creator God.

For an individual to grow from this perception, he has to understand the influences of his religion,culture - and others as well, to develop an awareness of each triggered belief and behaviours.

When an individual grows personal awareness, it limits one's quick and false judgements on other individuals who perceive to communicate with God in different ways beyond personal religious perspective.

Growing to understand that individual psychology on how to contact God was taught to him from his religious influences, and others were also taught their own different how in their religions as they followed the roots of religious leaders.

This knowledge can grow a being to understand that "the belief of an individual makes him behave accordingly since he understands the world that way".

And to grow one's spiritual perception, he should understand where and how he got his belief, and decide what to take or leave from what he knows.

Educational Perceptions

Resistance to knowledge

In this perception, a being never attends to influences that give more knowledge, and he resists change fearing mistakes, or believing that knowledge and talents which each different individual possess is fixed. As stated earlier by (Dweck 2017) as he showed how people with fixed mindsets resist new information due to their beliefs and perceptions.

A being with this mindset believes that knowledge and skills that one possesses are fixed and cannot grow beyond his perceived limitations. This belief however can lead an individual to avoid positioning thyself where there is new learning and self-improvement opportunity.

An individual becomes comfortable with what he knows, and if he encounters the threat of new information, it is created within him the urgency to try to prove himself over and over again even if he is wrong. This urgency to argue is created to defend one's ground and can lead to the development of an omniscient mentality in an individual.

Individuals with this perception also see failure as a threat that comes wrapped around new information. New information comes with new ways of thinking, new ways of doing things at work, and weigh out the old information and skills from an individual.

So, new information demand from an individual the ability to adapt and learn, trying to apply the new information through trial and error. However, with this perception, an error that is associated with practising this new psychology is perceived as a failure that can make a being feel vulnerable to change, and that perception may lead him to find it easy when he considers resisting change.

An individual with this perception considers resisting change since failure is a threat and enough de-motivator to him when it comes to trying anything new which might victimise him to change. This then leads him to view change as his greatest enemy and when change presents itself in his life and at work, he does not support it at all.

So, for him to grow from this perception, he should know that if a being watches the world getting past by without improving oneself, he will be left behind and becomes incompetent around the dynamic world.

For an individual's skills and ideas to become more competent in life or relevant to any business, he has to acknowledge information and seek more of it to grow in and from the sheep psychology.

Equivalent to group knowledge

As mentioned earlier, this is a skilled individual with talents hidden in dependent behaviours. A being with this perception possesses knowledge that is equivalent to group knowledge, and this influence normally creates a future that is not much different from spheres.

When an individual around group influences tries to develop new ways of doing things, he can however find himself trapped back into his old habits. This happens to him because changing behaviour from this perception requires a complete change of influences to create a different future.

After choosing to change an individual may start to feel uncomfortable as the new psychology (thinking and choosing independently) will not be his normal habit (following group choices and people's opinions).

So as he become to perceive his situation as hard and uncomfortable, he then ends up doing the same things which he used to do before, which can come up with the same predicted results. This grows him back into the sheep, a being who chooses to live a life which he may not like due to loss of confidence and becoming dependent on unpredictable future outcomes.

The eagerness of trying to know something alone will be perceived as a waste of time, leading to end up bringing group-based judgements and ideas to solve life situations.

These group-based perceptions may be biased and limited for an individual's growth, - making him lose most valuable opportunities in life since knowledge base is extracted from limited sources.

So, a being with this perception as long as he knows what his other friends know and do, he feels comfortable and secured around them.

This group equivalent knowledge makes him the sheep, as his confidence and independence to stand for himself is weakened whenever he comes up with something new or choosing something different in life. He might perceive that, after coming up with something new, his friends and family may not understand him and might not support his ideas.

This psychology however develops fear which leads a being to ask energy-draining questions like, "what if these desires fail?" or "what will people think of me?" or "what will people say?", and "what if this, what if that"…instead of thinking, "what if his own what if's work".

So, for a being to escape from these perceptions he should be willing to assess the ideas from his spheres and be willing to suggest his own best way of doing things while preparing for new challenges that demand his growth even if it may separate him from his spheres. This confidence grows his independence and willingness to normalise hard uncomfortable decisions that life might present to him.

As an individual grows to seek knowledge and improvement around his skills, his confidence will grow to become more independent when the time comes to make difficult life choices.

If individuals around him are unable to inspire him or help him to grow into his desires, he should find the courage to let them off from his new life.

As an individual grows to change his influences which made him be a sheep or influenced his undesired life before, he will grow to meet new stimuli from changed environment and spheres with the same psychology which he chooses to pick. Surrounding himself with individuals with the same perceptions as him, even when he loses motivation after a failure or negative energy, - he can grow back using the inspiration of his competitive company.

One might ask "how can I find a competitive company? my environment is too polluted for a being to grow from the sheep's perception!"

It is okay, the environment might be polluted but we have options to create our environment, and it has been made easier by the globalisation of social connections around the world as one person here! can choose his mentor or coach from a long distant country/region to grow him into his own desired goal. And it is easy to choose these influences, for example, take it as if you are scrolling down on your social media platform and discover that you are not finding what inspires you to be what you want to be in life. So instead of deleting the social platform to remove the undesired influences, you can choose to add what inspires you to be your dream, while on the other hand substituting influences that do not lead you to that dream.

Arguing to win (not for learning or better solution)

An individual with this perception always starts arguments with people, and what makes the argument tiring is that he keeps on raving without listening to others. When other individuals give their point of view which is different from what he has given, it causes more arguments, hatred, and tensions between individuals. The way a being who wants to win argues, can make him destroy relationships with people who might feel ignored from that given conversation.

When an individual with this perception is involved in an argument or decision making, he continues to pursue his main motive which is to win regardless of how limited his view might be. This however can lead him to argue unnecessarily till the other party is dragged into a fool's trap, as both parties might end up having unrelated discussion from the one which they wanted to discuss. This can cause some emotional conversations between parties leading to destructive arguments which are away from the solution. These arguments can cause conflicts and hatred between individuals or groups if one party cannot listen/refuse to consider the other party's views around the problem. This process can result in a lot of time being lost in arguments which at the end of the day do not provide a solid solution for the issue that may be presented.

An individual with this perception consumes a lot of time in arguments due to his urgency to try to prove himself over and over again, even if it is at the expense of the best outcome, causing more conflicts in his society and at work with colleagues.

In most instances when a person with this perception speaks, trying to continue arguing or answering his questions may lead the responder to seem more stupid (fool's trap) while keeping quiet around stupid arguments will make him feel smarter, which however makes it difficult to solve the fool's trap in a time-conscious situation.

So, a being should understand those stupid arguments rise when a being keeps on arguing about things he does not know, which exposes him more that he does not know the subject he is talking about. And to grow from this mentality he should admit the extend to which his knowledge and perceptions reach limits, and choose to become open to recognising knowledge which might help to grow his understandings or thoughtless actions.

When exposed to new information, one should be willing to listen and recognise self err while refraining from resisting knowledge.

…"As a being allow correction and learning from others, it helps to grow into knowing rather than showing foolishness in arguments."

Financial Perceptions

Money complications

An individual with the sheep financial perception does not understand money, he perceives that there is something intrinsically valuable around money. This perception of thinking that money is the value can lead him to chase money without even considering his talents for wealth creation. And when he hears people talking about this particular subject which is paying off these days, he can quickly jump onto the bus for the reason around how much money is involved.

Chasing money for the sake of money at the end of the day becomes tiring, making an individual unhappy even after accomplishing the desired amount of money. The worst part of an individual's money complications comes when he is reluctant to learn about how to manage money from a dime he gets since somehow he perceives the available amount of money to be too small for management. This causes money to always slip away from the individual's hands, even if he gets a bigger amount in the future, as the amount gets bigger, he might not understand the movement of his finances.

This inability to understand money can cause him to perceive that money is only stable in the hands of those who were born inheriting wealth, creating biased perceptions which neglect other many individuals in the world who started to work on their lives while building wealth from zero to great.

An individual with this perception thinks that the rich are very bad people and they rob him of his finances since he always finds himself getting poor and poor while the richer are getting richer.

So a growing individual from this perception should desire to grow his mindset from this perspective, to enhance an ability to see the difference between success momentum vs poverty momentum.

…"Success momentum is a process whereby an individual's efforts accumulates more opportunities for even more success", and "Poverty momentum is a process whereby an individual's previous unsuccessful life events accumulates due to lacking effort and persistence in one's visions which cause a being to be poorer in the future".

Between these lines that's when 1 realised how other people become to know more about money while others come to be vexed more by the topic. And the perceptions one has around his finances determine how he will use the money for himself and his future generation.

So grabbing financial awareness can help an individual to grow from the sheep into a being who can be able to make his own financial decisions, with the ability to understand reasons to why he is working when choosing to work for money, in the next chapter.

Miracle money?

An individual with this perception becomes lazy to think for himself on how to make big money that can cover his big dreams. He then chooses to demand miracles and free things from other people and God so that things can appear without reason or applied effort.

As a Christian most of the time when a church service is at its peak in spiritual influence when the pastor is standing in front of the congress and shouts 'receive your miracle!' to break an individual's life strongholds, the financial topic used to get my attention! drawing questions out of me like, "what am 1 receiving? the miracle its-self from the spiritual stimuli, like how Jesus fed thousand people with miracle fish and bread? or am 1 getting the blessings to flourish on every effort that 1 will be putting in every timed financial move?.

Then 1 grew to understand that the creator God does has his mysteries, and many areas for which all individuals may be privileged to learn, but growing from my spirituality out of these curiosities, 1 surely know that money from God does not appear like magic, but rather there should be an effort which comes wrapped around the blessing to get financial freedom.

So the miracle part around money comes after sweating, as related to the Christian bible story of Adam and Eve in the garden of Eden when God cursed Adam to sweat(work) to put food on the table in (Genesis 3:19)"..by the sweat of your brow, you will eat your food until you return to the ground,…"

Then 1 came to grow the understanding that, a being can also work his entire life without having any fruitful effort if he neglects to acknowledge his creator God. In this awareness, that's when 1 realised the importance of the miracle around wealth, as it comes indirectly like a blessing from the creator God to be fruitful like him, as per the creation of every human being.

…"Thus in this perception, a growing individual should understand that if he waits for a miracle to wealth without effort, it will not come."

Owing people money

A being with this perception might lack understanding around money, which can lead him to borrow large amounts of money from other people not having in mind the consequences of owing other people money. When he borrows money his intentions might be to serve his current problems but lacking financial awareness on what amount? why? when? and how to borrow money? can lead him astray.

Without financial awareness, an individual can end up working his entire life to cover debts becoming a servant to the ones to which he owes large amounts of money on which he pays large interests rates.

I used to read these stories from back in the ancient days where individuals who owed other people large amounts of money lost their freedom to life choices. They became obligated to pay off debts which they didn't even consider how much burden it will be in their lives, which detrimentally resulted in their property being seized, and those who had no collateral ended up being slaves to those which they owed. The worst part was that when they got enslaved by debts, their children were born slaves and their future generation giving birth to slaves from the mistakes of their father.

This situation is still relevant in modern society as the traditional banks, informal money lenders and other institutes are still willing to lend money to an individual who wants to use some of his future income presently for a vast number of purposes. If the debtor fails to repay as agreed, these creditors use their collateral securities and other penalties to gain possession of the money they owed the borrower.

So, those individuals who acquire large amounts of loans and mortgages might need to repay those obligations for a very long period, and the longer the time it will take for them to repay those loans, the more interest they will have to pay on the principal.

For an individual to grow from this perception of borrowing recklessly, he should develop financial awareness to know what amount? why? when? and how to borrow money? before making borrowing choices.

Under this, some individuals do avoid borrowing completely, some borrow recklessly and others borrow when it is needed.

Normally people who use loans to supplement their incomes by buying food, electricity, clothes and rent end up being trapped in the spiral of poverty and debt traps. So for a being to grow he should borrow money that he can repay and use it for purposes that makes him grow and happy.

For example, one wise being can use a loan to start a business and, or for education and training which is self-investment. Thus, for a being to be free from debt, he should avoid using loans for consumptive purposes and consider using them for business opportunities. And when he needs the money to borrow, he should compare the interests rates from available options and choose the best alternative.

Individual borrowing choices differ depending on their exposure from family, friends, to traditional banks and credit institutes depending on the amount of money, intended purposes, individual borrowing history and creditor's interest rates.

·········

Around Sheep Behaviours

I have seen many individuals switching from one church to another and when you ask them why doing so? they tell that the prophet from this church possesses more powers these days than the one in that church. This psychology then leads to a behaviour of moving between churches in search of miracles from church leaders, and when these individuals find themself meandering around on the same problem in their life? they switch to another church. At the end of the day, their life is stagnant and wonder if God exists, to answer their problems which may seem to be so confusing, as problems remain stuck on them like their shadows.

For an individual to substitute this behaviour of moving to the next big talk of the day, he should understand that God installed value in him which is hidden like treasure to seek and is expected by his creator God to create that value in his environment. Thus, if an individual is willing to unleash this value, he should have faith and believe in oneself, - if it happens that he fails, he should be willing to stand up without any second thought to search again.

...

As l grew up, I saw many individuals who did not finish what they have started because they did not know what to prioritise between the set plan and other distractions.

Another worst part comes when an individual has a particular idea in mind but does not possess the guts to start. I saw this in learning decisions, business ideas, and other life situations which require courage, persistence, and effort from an individual to manifest an idea. However, some individuals try to do something, for example, going to the gym, and or maintain health through diet then after few weeks they give up and go back to normal routines which take them to further away from their goals.

Then l looked at individuals accomplishing what they want, as they enjoyed those working processes which seemed painful in the eyes of those quitting and asked, "what is differentiating these people?". Within those curiosities, that's when l realised that individuals who quit do not have proper discipline and vision to accomplish something from the start. When they do something, they multi-task everything from overexercising to 100 business plans which are to be executed at the same time.

...

Also if an individual possesses the psychology that, "l don't deserve anything better in life" or "I can not fix this", he can give up in any situation, especially after a failure. And if an individual is trapped in this psychology, when he messes up, it will be difficult to view other life better choices to take other than the occupied mess up.

In this psychology, it is like there is no way back into something better, and the ease of thinking for another way out is consumed by regrets and fear. So for an individual to grow from this psychology of messing up, he should understand that 'most of the time as individuals we do mess up big time.

....when a being messes up! that's when others learn and grow while others become trapped under the same lesson on loop for a long time.

On the other hand, the individuals who learn from their mistakes find possible ways to live their lives by becoming more wise and experienced.

....

The Sheep Leadership

This is a virus l repeat! **a virus!!**, have you ever listened to the advice of a person and ask yourself where is this coming from? I do this sometimes, as I will be trying to figure out the motive around spoken words. And most times people who accomplished something are great motivators towards life, and when you find yourself around an individual who is afraid to try something because of failure, he can infect you with the same psychology.

Within this awareness that's when I realised that **"an utter from a wise man can flourish life and a gush from a foolish man can flounder life"**.

The title above is sheep leadership, yes! the sheep can lead, but when he leads, his followers suffer from fear, doubts, uncertainty, and lacking discipline about their future. This happens since a leader can transfer his energy to his followers and if that energy is negative, then every individual who feeds on that energy becomes energy drained from success.

One might ask, "so is this a fixed state? that when an individual perceives things or behave like the sheep, he is a complete sheep and can not change?".

Around the sheep, one needs to understand that for every individual on this planet to keep thyself from the sheep perceptions, - be persistent in maintaining and trying to be more understanding around influences of your actions. Practising how to become an independent thinker who does not allow any harmful contagious influences which might confuse individual intended goals.

When an individual forgets or stops to grow, he starts to attend to influences that divert his perceptions backward. This process leads him into an individual who manifests unproductive and harmful behaviours for himself and others in his environment.

The good news is this, 'an individual can put oneself in a state which helps to notice if his actions and behaviours are getting out of the track, by setting goals or a certain period which he should chronologically achieve'.

In this, if an individual is found around a hostile environment towards success or getting out of the track, he can easily detect the stimuli,- and now it is demanded within to find the courage to get back on the success track.

"When you follow a group of undedicated people, please remember!, 'The sheep leadership will lead you to that group destination, the destination of confused, undisciplined, defeated, and limited mindset"

....

Background Of Sheep Perceptions

An individual with this perception might have failed or has seen other individuals failing something which he used to believe was achievable. These past observed failures developed negative energy, fear, sadness, and giving up around his life and environment.

The past experiences which are filled with setbacks, lead a being to subtract thyself from something better in the future, - the uncertain future which requires bravery and faith in oneself.

Thus, fears reduce an individual's potential capabilities, hiding the potential in certain beliefs - like the fixed mentality around an environment.

Individuals around these influences are doubtful about the success of their ideas or projects in life. These doubts drain more of their energy and present failures, failures which manifest from feeling tired and procrastinating when it comes to working on targeted goals.

Now, let's step into the next chapter, **The Worker…**

Chapter 2

THE OX: "The secret to golden shekels is work"…(Babylon wisdom)

The worker

This is an individual who can perform manual labour for a living, contributing and add to the achievement of business objectives and possess the ability to work with others in a group setting.

A worker's psychology

An individual with the Ox psychology believes in working! he perceives that 'if a being does not work, there will be no food on his table'. This belief helps him to work hard to provide himself and his family with essentials such as food and clothes.

Normally an individual with this psychology is a breadwinner of the family and is determined to put the prominence of his family in his work. He can even request overtime at work to get extra money, to cover up his current and future financial obligations. His financial awareness differentiates him from someone who wants free things into a being who wants to add his time value in return for financial compensation. Compensation is his main motive to work hard since getting compensated makes him feel happy and motivated to be more productive. However, most individuals with this psychology end up following companies that are offering better income than crucial career development. Mind, this is throwing oneself back into the sheep psychology by becoming an individual who just follows the money for the sake of how much money is involved at a particular work.

An individual may come to follow the money in this psychology since in most instances having that money can help to solve current, and future financial problems without delay of talent search in oneself. This talent negligence, however, traps by believing in other individuals with a position above and or bosses to determine one's worth around individual desperate searches.

As mentioned earlier, a being with the OX psychology is a hard worker but his perceptions around perfection normally ruin his work since he is not eager to try something new that has a high possibility of failure. This desire for perfection was taught to him at school as he saw individuals who made mistakes being punished. Leading him into a being who always plays it safe in life by perceiving mistakes as unacceptable, and a great threat when it comes to performing something new at work.

His mentality somehow still possesses a negative self-concept around his own beliefs, leading him to view himself as a dependent being who cannot make it without being employed in life.

So, these fears lead him to avoid other career opportunities which might require his talents and independence, like starting his side ventures outside employment.

In most cases, individuals with this psychology were influenced by their undesirable financial background, and when they look back into that poor financial background, present life becomes a blessing - a blessing on which they are grateful to have.

You can hear them saying, "as long as I can pay my bills and provide my family with essentials, I am okay!".

Spiritual Perceptions

Praying in action

(Mathew 7:7/Luke 11:9) "Ask and it will be given to you, seek and you will find, knock and the door will be opened to you"

Most individuals in this group are grateful for what they have and thank God for what he has done for them in their lives. So they pray and take action by working towards what they want in life. While they pray to God for him to hear their prayers, they put some effort towards the achievement of their desires.

If it occurs that they fail, they get up and pray until actions find a breakthrough into their desires.

This perception helps an individual to develop faith in his actions perceiving that God will answer his prayers, and all he needs to do is keep on knocking. He understands that if he only prays for the miracle to come true without placing himself where the miracle can meet him, nothing will happen in his life. So he seeks for his desires through actions aligned with prayers, and when he doesn't know what to do next in life, he asks for his God to help him with strength and guidance.

An individual with this perception knows that miracles are there and may come in life as opportunities that find seeking individuals. 'Seeking individuals' who ask for a miracle to come through, while knocking at the door which is believed to hold individual desire.

In this spiritual perception, a being can see the wonders of God in oneself since prayers which were acted upon before in life were answered, believing "miracles to be in every individual's hustle".

…" miracles come in different forms and sometimes they come through people who present information, gifts and opportunities."

Financial Perceptions

Working for money

Individuals with this perception are aware that money does not fall from trees like leaves, so they are willing to work for their financial needs and breakthroughs in life.

They seek employment to provide labour and in return given compensation for their work.

When they want extra cash they can work extra hours to cover up their financial obligations and needs. So, these individuals are determined to get money through work, providing their lives with what they want.

However, when they get money, fear of losing that money on investments leads them to refuse investments options but rather choose savings. This leads the worker to work without investment plans since he perceives these investments to be too risky. Somehow, debts keep reminding the individual that if he stops working, his income will stop, and will be left with only obligations which he has to meet every month. So the only option he has is to keep on working tirelessly to cover those bills and expenses.

To grow in and from this perception, one should understand that money can be used to work for you by making more of its descendants in the future through investments. The question that may come to mind is how can money work for an individual in this modern world? well! continue reading below and into the following chapters stepping each staircase towards leadership.

At each staircase, it is made for a being to understand how each individual and his animal resemblance perceive life, with knowledge about what it takes to be in their shoes from personal beliefs to associated behaviours in different situations.

Saving money

In this financial perception, we have individuals who save money for their children for school, family, and other essential future use. Savings meet their future needs and cover them when they are money short. These savings can also be used to build or buy something when the money they have been bringing up is now able to meet the price tag. Saving is a great approach and is encouraged for every individual to have a certain amount of money they are willing to save every month.

However, if a being desires growth from this perception, he should seek more knowledge around hedging on the saved money. And he should know that when a large amount of money is saved doing nothing for the individual it is now called "dead money, or idle money". Dead money is the money which when you can go, and come back after months or years, you will find it the same or diminishing.

The growth in financial perception needs an individual to know that when he gives time to an organisation in return for financial needs, he should be able to make that money grow in the future.

Saving is not a bad idea since you can get some interest through saving your money in the bank, but while an individual is saving his money he should have in mind the way on how to grow his money. Having options in mind on investments develops awareness in the individual to seek wise choices which might get his interest.

Fear of losing ... A person in this mentality saves money because he is afraid that he might lose his money if he tries to invest it. So he chooses to save money till it is enough to buy what he wants in his life. He perceives investing as too risky and prefers to keep his money where he can find it the exact way he left it.

To grow in this perception, a being should understand that losses exist in business and to grow? seek knowledge about where you want to put your money, to decrease any chances of losing that money when you take risks.

> " if you fail, you will gain experience and more knowledge to be able to cover those failures in the future with advanced and improved approaches."

Money as the root of all evil

In this perception, an individual believes that " the love of money is the root of all evil", he however works for money and is motivated by it at work through promotion and high salary but he associates money with evil, and unethical behaviours.

In this perception, a being knows that money is power, and is aware that power can corrupt. He even noticed people growing into riches by taking shortcuts at the expense of others in society and developed a mentality that rich people very are evil. Even if he wants money to satisfy his own different future needs, his psychology however keeps on associating the motive to become rich with unethical behaviours.

To grow in this perception, an individual should admit that he loves money and wants to be rich since he works for money. Money was discovered to be his best motive which enhances his work performance (Locke, Feren, McCaleb, Shaw, and Denny, 1980).

In this perception, a worker should be willing to make money ethically, legally, and wisely to get even high income through promotion and high salary.

Money is important for happiness to an individual if he achieves in life, he gains respect around him and power to decide his own will.

Since he perceives that money is power, and power corrupts. He should grow perceptions on how money can be used nobly if one possesses it. Understanding the ancient wisdom suggests, that *'no one can take money to the grave'*, thus, people should give money to charities, donations and do many good deeds with it.

' the virtuous are those who, despite their love for it, give away their wealth to their relatives and orphans and the very poor, and to travellers and those who ask for charity, and to set slaves free'.The Holy Quran(Heifer 2:177)

Educational Perceptions

Going to school for hire

In this psychology, an individual perceives going to school as a key to open his employment security. The desire to be hired lead him to attend school, learning a particular program so that after completing the process he can be hired.

At work, he can also upgrade his education to increase his chances of being promoted and compensated appealingly.

In this perception, a being can choose which area he wants to work on and then go to school to learn new necessary skills to be able to get the targeted employment. However, some individuals with this perception are influenced by the society and spheres to make choices rather than looking from within them to find their abilities and interests which they need to grow.

So, if a being desires growth in and from this perception, he should choose a profession to be hired in which is aligned with his purpose and or career development. A being can find his purpose and individual answers from within him, and if he however makes choices due to what other people are thinking for him then his psychology is covered with the sheep.

To make independent choices and before deciding, an individual should ask oneself a couple of questions which should help to check if he is being authentic,

self-check list,

➢ why am l choosing this?

am l best at doing this?

do l enjoy doing this?

will I get my passion through this?

➢ what is my future in this?

These questions give an individual an overview when it comes to identifying the stimuli which caused him to choose certain choices, and will have in mind what he will gain beyond making a life choice. However, in this case, the negligence of one's ability and negative self-concept can cause a being to undermine his independence and value.

So, If an individual chooses a profession because someone else is making money in that particular area, he can end up doing what he is not good at or doing what he does not like, the job becoming a burden in his life even if it has a high income.

"For a being to grow in and from this perception he should understand that money is everywhere as long as you are in the right treasure hunt career, a career which you enjoy doing."

Learning for titles

In this educational perception, an individual believes in titles, for him to qualify into a particular position. He understands that for a being to be recognised at a certain position, he has to be qualified. This helps him to desire learning and attend growth into a more qualified individual. After an individual successfully attains the required job qualifications, he becomes confident to apply for his desired work title. However, titles may create discrimination in society if a being stereotypes other people as inferior who did not choose to reach a certain level of education.

This perception can lead a person to entitle himself at work and society, boasting about how educated he is, and showing how small he views other people who did not achieve what he has in life.

When an individual believes in titles too much, his interpretations of other people's abilities become biased since he perceives himself to be more intelligent than others. So, when other people provide their thoughts, he may think that it's an uneducated decision and will withdraw his attention.

" the world is demanding creative people, not people who are entitled since a title cannot solve a situation unless an individual who possesses the title knows how."

Learning to avoid mistakes

Individuals with this perception fear making mistakes because there were taught that if a person makes mistakes he gets punishment. This fear can develop him into a being who wants to play it safe avoiding uncertain ideas and actions at his work and in life.

In this perception, a being learned to avoid mistakes at school during preparation to fit for a company and was told that 'when you make a mistake at work you will be fired'. He was taught this in such a way that punishes failing students and rewards perfect students. "I still remember when I was in high school, my English teacher would beat you and or embarrass you in front of everyone for using wrong spellings in a composition writing, ignoring the fact that a student is trying. Then in the next composition essay? I would personally write few vocabularies which I was 100% sure about and repeat them till my essay is complete. It sounded absurd but why would someone try to get the price of being embarrassed or get whipped in experimenting?

This fear of making mistakes grows in the individual till he gets into his own business or at work in an organisation. He will not be innovative because of fears around what people will think of him if he comes up with an idea that might be viewed as stupid.

These fears can limit an individual from growing into a being who possesses the ability to manage his limitations and other people at work. Fear limits an individual when it comes to creating new ways of production in the company, perceiving that when someone makes a mistake, the company will fire and or punish for mistakes.

So, to grow from this perception, an individual should understand that the limits to own success are in one's mind and modern companies are demanding employees who are creative and confident.

" making mistakes helps an individual to learn and do better the next time, leading the organisation which he works for into progress around innovations rather than being stagnant in its current and future operations."

··········

Recall: **Perception Stimuli**

Most people with this perception came from educated families, or around spheres with the belief of getting good grades in school, to be employed for a better position by reputable organisations. This influence leads an individual to work hard in school for hire, by a company that provides equivalent or high income to individuals who reached certain heights in traditional education.

The society which develops these perceptions views the impact of each individual's decision on a certain topic to be determined by the heights of his traditional education and, or his financial support.

So, individuals strive to be recognised as valuable by their families and around society. This then creates the motive to impress other people and, certain distress sensations on the individual around other people's opinions and judgements.

………

The stimuli around individual fears when it comes to investments has been influenced by seeing many people losing money through these investments. And on the other hand, noticing some individuals who did not invest, securing their money in savings and pension plans for future retirement.

This experience influenced their decision to always have something on which they can fall back on (savings), in times of economical downturns and currency devaluations which can result in losing funds from investments.

……...

Ox spiritual-finance perceptions are also influenced by religious beliefs as an individual grows up being told that… " the love of money is the root to all evil", developing within the unwillingness to desire money in excess. This influence results in diminishing efforts from an individual as he comes to settle for an average life or do nothing to build his financial goals.

…………

Other Behaviours

Individuals with the ox-perceptions are great contributing team members in an organisation and society. They are good at achieving assigned duties and responsibilities from their counterparts and supervisors at work. This gives confidence to the management of a company as they become willing when involving employees in challenging tasks.

The management perceives that the worker likes to work and will be able to perform work while requiring little supervision around that given task. This also may help the worker to be given opportunities for decision making, towards certain organisational operations since he has field experience and is willing to accept new challenges.

These types of workers are perceived by the management as loyal and self-driven when it comes to accomplishing organisational goals.

However, management perceives that not everyone likes to work, some individuals dislike working. These perceptions led to the formulation and application of Douglas McGregor theories **Y** and **X**. The formulation of theory **Y** and theory **X** is based on the two controversial aspects of human behaviour at work. These aspects then provide a manager's perception around different employees at work based on various assumptions through their behaviours.

Oh, tighten up your brain belts buddy, it's getting intellectual here!

In summary, theory **Y** assumes that employees like to work and are more committed, and are more loyal when given appealing compensations and rewards. In this perception, an employee who likes to work is given chances for growth, and development in career development since the behaviour of liking work is likely to help an individual to grow into the next chapter 'the competent manager'.

It is perceived that he grew from the ability to manage himself, into the ability to manage resources towards the success of an organisational objective.

This person must be cool right? self-management to organisational management. I wanted to be like this growing up. Okay, let's go back! Where was I?

Then theory **X** assumes that employees dislike work and are unwilling to take responsibility. In this perception around behaviours of the worker, there is no trust between a manager and the worker. The management believes that an employee who dislikes working, will avoid work if possible, and for an employee who dislikes work to be productive, he must be controlled and threatened with punishment around his lousy behaviours.

The manager is what we are growing in to right now but he is still managing us, right? Yeah in his mind, so let's recall how he perceives the worker, to help the worker's growth.

·······

Behaviour Conclusion

An individual with the Ox perception likes to work (theory **Y**) and is committed to his work. However, many influences can lead a worker to dislike work, for example, a being facing long financial obligations, or other unpleasant internal and external influences blah blah blah!.

These unpleasant influences can make the workplace no longer feel like a place to grow, but rather a place to work! which is tiring for the employee.

Who wants to feel like this anyway? Let's take the prescription.

"a growing employee should understand how to manage unpleasant internal and external influences which might affect an organisation's productivity."

...how? continue reading.

....

Growth of worker's perceptions

In the leadership journey, an individual should learn new skills and knowledge to grow into a being who can manage himself, and other resources towards success.

So, the following awareness can help a worker to grow competent in the organisation and or start a business. That's the birth of being cool buddy.dig,

Creative ability

Creative scholars discovered that within everyone there is creative ability and people are creative daily in their lives and at work even if they do not recognise that they are being creative. Creative ability grows when a being comes up with designs, artifacts, objects that are both (new, original, fresh...) with the ability to be productive, useful and creating value to others. If someone comes up with something creative, it should fit the context and the purpose which it is intended to save.

An individual who grows this ability can solve the 21-century business problems and challenges of turning information into inventiveness, leading to the rise of businesses that demand creative thinkers for growth around industrial innovations.

However, this creative ability is vulnerable to an individual marginalized in traditional education, since traditional education's structures are based around certainty, grades and single answer thinking. Daniel Pink illustrated the increasing value of creative abilities when he stated that …' Today, the defining skills of the previous era- the "left brain" capabilities that powered the information age - are necessary but no longer sufficient. And the capabilities we once disdained or thought frivolous - the "right-brain" qualities of inventiveness, empathy, joyfulness, and meaning -increasingly will determine who flourishes and who flounders'.

With the above awareness, a being grows to ignite the willingness to experiment with new things and think outside the box for value creation. Growing his attention on situations that need to be solved and modified in the environment and business.

Creative ability grows an individual's focus to perform work while anticipating the greater goal of his organisational operations.

So, growing more into an individual who is not afraid to fail, but rather sees the greater price beyond fear of trying something brings joy after success.

Now go create something, you know you possess the ability, try!

Self Confidence

This awareness comes around by defining self-efficacy as -the beliefs, perceptions that one possesses on himself around the ability to complete a certain task (Foley, Kidder, and Powell 2002).

Wait, my brain is *zhizhing*, lets read that again!

Yeah now let's go'…When a worker is given a task to perform, it is the confidence that makes him perform the delegated task using skills which he already possesses to complete it. This confidence also opens room for him to learn new information and skills at work, leading him to support change in the organisation.

You are getting it right?

Self-confidence makes an individual view change as achievable in life /the organisation, and become comfortable when the organisation is initiating change, influencing further the degree to learn new information and skills at the workplace. This confidence helps an individual to share complex information and to stand up in groups,…also opening new opportunities for leadership transformation.

So, a worker who is not confident does not support learning new information and skills since he is afraid of potential failures from tried experiments. He sees change as a threat to his career and does not support it in the organisation. This makes him a stagnant individual in his career, who is a liability to the organisation.

Not cool at all…..!

To grow in and from this perception, a worker needs to understand the importance of growing his confidence in his career.

…. confident individuals are willing to take on challenging tasks and roles which improves the way they perceive their new environment. Individuals with this ability grow into beings who can solve situations without self-doubt and are willing to take the next challenging task at work. Why?

They understand that tasks are different and require different methods to approach, so, they learn new methods which are unfamiliar to gain more experience and confidence in the future.

In business confident workers are willing to go the extra mile in achieving corporate objectives and their personal goals. Differentiating them from an individual who has a low level of confidence, who is shy and unsure of oneself, and is more likely to avoid tasks which he perceives uncertain.

At work, a confident person has faith in what he does, making himself a theory Y type of employee, to whom the manager is eager to give more responsibilities and opportunities for appraisals and promotions.

He is getting cooler, the manager is thinking about giving him his job?. **Huh?** In your dreams Simba you are not yet ready. But you are close,

Listening skills

Listening involves paying attention to and the ability to interpret, assigning meaning, remembering and analyse the presented.

Training managers felt that poor listening was one of the most important problems facing them and that ineffective listening leads to ineffective performance and low productivity (Hunt and Cusella, 1983).

An individual should understand that listening is important for his productivity, (Haas and Arnold 1995) stated …"a growing body of research suggests that listening ability or the perception of effective listening, is inextricably linked to effective individual performance in an organisation".

So, training is required for a being to learn how to give feedback and how to ask questions at work. However, for the ability to come out of oneself, an individual should be motivated to do so.

An individual should make more time around studying the topic of listening and training needed at the workplace, to be able to incorporate listening skills and use them to make judgements of others at the workplace. However, one should bear in mind that listening in the work environment is different from listening in the classroom environment due to different variables.

What is going on now? so how do we do it?.,

For an individual to improve his work listening skills, he

should include four of (Kippen and Green 1994) active listening techniques. Techniques which includes,

(1) restating or paraphrasing a message,

(2) summarising the main issues of a conversation,

(3) acknowledging and verbalising non-verbal messages,

(4) responding to feelings that may be expressed.

To do this effectively, one can use the active listening process by (Hoppe 2007) suggesting his six-step process: "active listening involves six skills, paying attention, holding judgement, reflecting, clarifying, summarizing, and sharing".

Regardless of the technique or skill at the workplace, all authors about listening agreed on its importance at the workplace for the growth of an individual from being a worker into leadership.

So, listening abilities can help an individual while he works with others as a group, for example when one individual is trying to express how he views the situation and how to solve it. A growing individual set his difference aside and listen to the validity of other individual's suggestions before trying to be heard. This improves the quality of feedback that he gives to his counterparts, and increasing the team productivity on the assigned task.

If this skill is short, an individual jumps to conclusions when others are talking and is likely to perform delegated tasks in the wrong way. So, growing listening ability enables an individual to listen actively to clients, family, superiors and solve their problems.

When people around an individual feel heard, they develop a strong relationship with the individual in society and at work.

So, making other people feel understood is the key to growth and success, putting aside the push of trying to be heard as an individual.

"People will learn from you, listen to you, love you, buy from you and hire you,…when they feel understood not when they understand you." **Dean Graziosi**

Self-management

This refers to the continuous process of managing, evaluating and reinforcing our actions, thoughts, and emotions to have appropriate behaviours or performance in relation to our surroundings and environment through constantly reminding ourselves of our norms and values (Goleman et al, 2002).

Around this, that's when the environment notices some growing leadership qualities in you Simba. Ahuh! In you, self-managed being.

Well, we all have different personalities, wants and needs and different ways of showing our emotions, and when an individual prioritise the values, and norms of where he is working, he can grow to self manage himself to align his behaviours towards the achievement of the organisational goals. However, the organisation and an individual may have different values and visions, so self-management is a necessity for a being to internalise the organisational values to become productive.

This self-management is in form of self-regulatory, and if an employee self-regulatory fails at work, his thoughts, feelings and behaviours are driven by emotional immediate stimuli, (Renn et al 2011) leading a being to harm the goals of an organisation.

So, a person should practise the self-management process at work and in his personal life through goal-setting, self-monitoring, self-assessment and self-reinforcement. In this process, an individual becomes aware of important goals, his progress in achieving the goals, and ways to get back if the momentum is lost.

Igniting behaviours which can help to reach individual goals, while avoiding other behaviours which do not benefit the accomplishment of these goals.

An individual growing this skill should understand that self-management gives awareness of what will happen if personal behaviour is not aligned with the organisational goal, which is poor employee productivity.

An organisation is effective if its employees can produce the expected output levels within the expected time frame. So, self-management helps the employee to work actively and encourage oneself to be more independent and finish delegated tasks in time-conscious situations.

A self-managed individual understands what he is supposed to do at a particular time, and can manage his life in a certain discipline towards achieving his goals. This individual can see the essence of time and is willing to improve oneself to manage time aligned with the use of resources in a productive way.

In this quality a being is perceived as self-disciplined in life and at work from his commitment, to make targeted goals a success personally and professionally.

Bonus perception,

✓ *Being-humble*

In brief, if a worker grows to be humble, he develops the eagerness to prove value in life by showing efforts rather than going around boasting about life accomplishments. Growing to understand the importance of other people's efforts, differences, and even grow to become someone who appreciates others.

With this awareness an individual can try to improve the impact of actions more than words, understanding that words without actions are empty.

With these skills, an individual can open new opportunities in a profession, and the list is endless to a hard-working individual who is willing to go the extra mile in life.

Now, you are ready to go further into management!…

Chapter 3

The Elephant: "When there is no enemy within! the enemy outside, can do us no harm"…(African Proverb)

The competent manager

This is an individual who possesses the ability to organize people and resources towards the effective pursuit of the organisational future objective.

Psychology Of the Elephant

The elephant believes that anything is possible if a being strongly manages the situation towards success. When he works to achieve something, he possesses a lock-pick type of mentality which makes him see a way through even if there is uncertainty, and hates it when someone tells him that this goal is impossible.

He believes in himself to be a person who can do something big if given enough resources to accomplish a plan. This helps him to give feedback to people who own these resources while requesting what he wants to achieve his goals at work. When given required resources for work to progress, he believes in following the organizational tradition by managing these resources with uniforms from the past company's operations.

The elephant believes that he is strong when it comes to solving business current obstacles, which demand more positiveness, while on the other hand, seeking advise from superiors for guidance, and wisdom in the management area. This gives him the strength to organize resources with motivation when operating on different challenges which might drain energy from him and the people he supervises. However, under his supervision, he believes to be the existence of other employees who dislike work, so he does not normally trust employees to work in his absence. Leading him to be all over the place, sweating to meet deadlines, and sometimes at the expense of his subordinates.

So in business, an individual with the elephant's psychology tells thyself that 'you have to be where your work is, to be successful'. This mindset triggers the behaviour of monitoring tightly when people are working around him, believing that his presence prevents bottlenecks at work.

Remember! last time we talked about the manager things got intellectual, that's who he is, his background is built around knowledge, so as you noticed in the last chapter on the growing worker.

...don't worry we are going to make it simple, sticking it in with a hedgehog approach!

Educational perceptions

Formal education's importance

The elephant believes that his most fundamental break in life was made by the rewards which he got by attending a traditional school. School gave him information that is industrial related, and a background in his perception about how a workplace is supposed to look like. At work his ability to turn information into action will be his authentic test, to prove that he can further extend the knowledge he possesses by managing different practical industrial situations.

So going to school for him is gaining the know-how of the industry and developing his career while being given a title or certificate as a passport to get employment. So he knows that to be hired, his passport is a level of education from a formal school. Recruiters seek employees who can assure their return on the investment. So if they see high grades from an individual's schooling background they perceive him to possess the information and ability to learn quickly in the industry.

That's why companies request a CV furnished with certificates, experiences and, then interview selected individuals who might possess the skills and knowledge to fit in the organization.

Informal education's importance

The elephant perceives that informal education is important for his growth and development. His growth into a competent manager was developed by some of the experiences in which he grew from personal learning, through being coached and mentored.

In this perception a being knows that formal education is important but not enough for his leadership success, Yah traditional school is not enough.

An individual should seek more information around personal dreams and profession to become more of a competent manager.

So, knowledge from informal education, helps an individual to be more competitive in the industry, by being able to handle difficult situations with extended knowledge, skills and confidence.

Formal + informal education

An individual with growing educational perceptions perceives that there is a strong connection between formal and informal education. Using formal education to develop a personal career through learning industrial background and attaining required certificates which secure employment.

Informal education then strengthens the profession by creating a reputation of a being who is competent in the industry with information, and the abilities aligned with the current and future business demands.

Absorbing this perception allows an individual to learn something from school, but not allowing it to interrupt individual informal education.

In this psychology, an individual is aware that, what is learned from school is not one's limitation for growth but rather the beginning for self-value creation and career development.

We need some spirituality now!....

Spiritual perceptions

Groom your spirituality

(2 timothy 1:7)For God did not give us a spirit of timidity, but a spirit of power, of love, and self-discipline

An individual should understand the importance of spiritual growth, to develop persistence and positive thinking at work. So the elephant perceiver grows his spirituality through taking actions to achieve a certain plan, and after accomplishing it, he gains more energy and confidence to accept new challenges.

This energy which is generated by previous success then becomes the byproduct to do more actions.

He also understands grooming of spirituality as the ability to follow required discipline with loyalty at work. When given a certain situation to manage, it is demanded within him to set aside his interests and prioritize the goals of his work.

So, spirituality grows within an individual, in form of patience and tranquillity towards achieving the business vision. This spiritual grooming helps in life to manage individual beliefs, and how to behave, showing discipline in different situations. He might find himself in situations at work which he used to personally quit or get emotional, but when a being encounter that situation at work it takes a groomed spirit to manage those emotions.

Remember self-management?....we are here!

This perception grows an individual to know the different demands in different situations with expected behaviours from an individual.

So, as an individual's spirituality grows, one begins to understand even more about personal beliefs and actions, managing those beliefs and actions to perform like a successful manager.

As he grows to manage his spiritual perceptions, he gains the ability to lead others, developing new beliefs about other people and their behaviours. Like for example, a manager who practise tight control systems at the work…..This is triggered by the belief that 'you have to be where your work is' and 'employees dislike work'. So, this particular perception grows one's psychology into a manager who wants progress from others, perceiving to find it through strict monitoring…..**Note!,** this particular perception can grow.

Financial perceptions

Managing finances

The competent manager understands knowledge of financial management as important towards the success of an individual career. He studied how to manage a business and his finances to grow value by avoiding miscalculated risks.

This helped him to understand the relationship between risk and desired return, being aware of how to choose between investments which he perceives to be profitable. When he analyses the return from risk to be too risky he changes his financial decision and chooses the next better investment option. So, analyzing these financial decisions increases the chances of winning in his investments and business.

As financial perceptions grow through informal or formal education, an individual learns other wise ways of growing personal income, avoiding expenditure on things that reduces cash flow. "Cash flow is the amount of money that is left in an individual's account after removing liabilities, monthly expenses and taxes".

This knowledge helps an individual to avoid increasing liabilities which makes him obligated to payoff on monthly interest for a long period.....I guess the game Rate Race taught me some financial moves!...

So though he tries to avoid liabilities as from his formal financial education, he literary buy liabilities perceiving them to be assets. He, however, finds those perceived assets taking money from him monthly reducing his cash flow for other investment opportunities. A house mortgage, car loan, house properties, and other miscalculated investments are examples of liabilities that can reduce disposable cash flow.

I thought there were assets too in school, my teacher told

me….maybe he lied or maybe he didn't know or just following the tradition…unlearn that buddy!

So, to grow financial management, an individual needs to understand personal cash flow more by analyzing which, from the desired properties gives him more money, and which ones are reducing personal monthly income….that's it, I learned my new lesson and it's shared.

Mentored to invest

A competent manager is a being who understands the importance of seeking mentors who guide him to learn about how to invest money. He manages to study smart investors who have experience in areas that got his interests and learn from their investing experience.

Learning to master the ways which experts use to analyse market situations and their shared discipline, before deciding to put money. His financial mentor for example might have written something or got interviewed about his financial interest, for example 'how to invest in stocks' and then shared skills and discipline which they perceived to be important to grow an individual from being a dummy to an expert.

In this perception, an individual takes advise from experts since he knows that experienced individuals know what made them lose or win in their previous investments, and might provide information about how to avoid losing money when another individual invest in that similar interest.

Selling value

The competent manager understands the creation of value as important in life and in products that he intends to sell for financial returns. He perceives that- 'when people buy goods which you are selling or involving you into their business they will be after the value you provide'.

This develops his eagerness to attend to information that grows value within, to enable his ability to manifest that value in his work. In this perception, an individual desires to increase the value of his provisions to targeted clients and superiors by keeping them satisfied with his work. His work is what he sells to get finance since he perceives that money comes after value,... and to get more finances a being needs to put more effort into what he does to elevate value in his provisions.

Within this perception, an individual perceives that customers desire different things in life, and the ability to sell a provision that caters for most of the market makes the business a success.

So, this awareness helps him to add value to what he is selling by changing his targeted customer perceptions in form of advertisements about current and or upcoming products. Also changing their perceptions when the business has been through bad publicity which is perceived to reduce sales in the future.

Well, these processes make customers understand struggles which the business has been through when it was creating the product. As customers see the struggle through adverts and how good it is intended to be, they will perceive the product's value.

....these adverts about a product which came from south of Africa to north of America, with struggles like wind and hurricanes, almost losing the product. The point? just to catch the emotions of customers to perceive the value.

So around this, a competent manager can also show value by providing customers with inventions,....showing those customers how the invention is substituting the old ways of doing things while showing the value that is being added to customers when they choose that product.

So, you are good at advertising now? But for you to be a successful manager, the customers who buy those products should be satisfied to have more positive testimonies, boosting the confidence of other potential customers. Well, having them coming back again!

Ummm, good ideology right?… let's see how he came to think like this, maybe you want to be like so.

....

Recall: **Perception Stimuli**

This perception was born from the desire aligned with an ability to manage resources in life and business. This made an individual understand that to grow in and from the Elephant perception, one has to accept responsibilities. As the saying goes ..."great power comes with more responsibilities", thus, "with more responsibilities comes great power", to grow even more responsibilities and so on.

In these desires, the competent manager was trained and natured to manage resources in business and life relating situations. This awareness enhanced the manager's view on setbacks around work and life, creating the ability to manage situations while differentiating himself from an ordinary worker.

....

At work

In this psychology, an individual is aware of the actions of his employees at work, while meeting the deadlines of his superiors and customers. To meet these deadlines, he implements tight control systems which makes it easy to control the movements of a subordinate for maximum productivity in his department.

As we stated earlier, this behaviour can also help to monitor (theory X) type of employee by Douglas McGregor, (an employee who dislike work), by keeping the employee's actions aligned with the organisational mission.

Sometimes an employee is hired and fails to return a profit to the organisation, the competent manager steps in to increase the production of each individual by assisting and monitoring employee movements.

In this psychology, the manager develops tactical goals and set a plan to reach that goal, through delegation…continuing to monitor and assisting the operation.

When a competent manager sets tactical plans in the organisation, he is demanded to grow patience around his employees. This patience can help to tolerate employees when they request favours from him at work and in their personal lives. He grows to become a sensitive being towards other peoples feelings by developing concerns about the triggers of their behaviours at work, and then influence employee's psychology by tapping into their emotions, showing empathy to increase their productivity at work.

This is the basic, let us dig into the growth!

"It's important that you grow because if you don't! you die, a serious death of ignorance……"

Elevated Manager

For an individual to grow in and from the elephant perception, he should set **high standards** to reach targeted goals. These high standards give employees a certain measure for comparative evaluations between success and failure in the organisation, Giving them the view of expected quality on their performance at work.

This behaviour of setting high standards show employees the bigger picture of the manager's intentions and gives them an understanding of why they are working,....having in mind the expected results from their efforts.

.... "people work with motivation when they know where they are going", and for them to achieve these high standards, a competent manager should grow into a being who can **set clear goals** around set standards,....goals which are **very simple and brief** for others to understand.

In this psychology, there is a need to show employees the organisational goals with **confidence**, and the ability to **communicate expectations** in achieving these goals while monitoring to see if employees are performing good or bad around stated measurements.

.....when employees know what is expected to achieve the delegated goals, they work with morale, following the boundaries created by the manager's expectations in the operation.

After setting high standards, a growing manager then **teaches others effectively** to be ready for the future and uncertain situations. Teaching others new skills and knowledge for them to develop confidence at work when they face difficult situations, by recalling their training to overcome.

Well, there is still a need to assist employees when they need help, developing **patience** around monitoring their performance while they try to put their information into practice.

A growing manager in this elevation **makes listening a priority** from his workers and his superiors, to keep them feel heard as he develops strong relationships from the top to the bottom of the organisational structure.

We talked about this in the previous chapter, practise how to master listening skills at constant....its so important.

For more light, an individual can show that he is listening to others by attending to them without any distractions around, like putting cell-phone aside and other accessories.

This attention boosts personal understanding of the topic, also making others feel heard as they express their feels. I guess you should know that,... when people express themselves they come up with different opinions and suggestions which might be very important for the business and individual growth. Helping you to recognise your own bias on the way you perceive things and accept other individuals points of view, regardless of their post in the business....and society of course!

So, when you master the ability to listen, people get motivated to feedback on the positive and even negative situations in an organisation. When there is negative feedback from others, a competent manager should be able to attend to it by giving others motivation and showing them possibilities of winning the situation.

...a manager for keeps over here!...

As people get used to feedback, they build trust around the manager, demanding from him more paid attention and appropriate responses.

Building trust at work helps you to develop team spirit around other colleagues, making other individuals work together with fewer conflicts. However, when conflicts arise....**they are inevitable!** so the competent manager should be able to resolve conflicts between individuals by understanding their different behaviours and perspectives. Solving these conflicts by showing other individuals the importance of business mission than their interests and egos at the workplace, and then teach them to learn within to put their differences aside…., teaching others to manage, you see?

So, when other individuals show efforts to resolve these conflicts let's say, and put the organisation as a priority, a competent manager should show credibility for their efforts even if it might seem small for the organisational success….its big, they will do more to prioritise the business.

…" small steps get us closer to the main destination, acknowledge them".

(5) Bonus tip……

As you grow to understand other people's different behaviours and perspectives, you should be able to learn to take diplomatic approaches when approaching targeted goals….why?

Diplomatic approaches help an individual to put ego aside when important decisions are being made by other individuals, even if it might make you feel inferior.

It is demanded within you to learn to use logic and reasoning when making decisions, to see facts and their importance rather than emotionally attached decisions. If however, you find yourself losing your diplomatic approach?, revise it by attending to the stimuli which made you able to use logical decisions before.

….note, this is a good stimulus to re-read for gaining back diplomatic approach. **Remember!** ego aside.

So, for an individual to grow from the elephant perception, one should monitor personal consistency, with awareness of the consequences if it is ceased. ??? Everything falls bad for re-build.

Before we get into the next chapter, let's discuss what might limit an individual to perceive things like a competent manager or to grow further into leadership.

....

Barriers to growth

Fear is the main barrier for an individual's growth to manage a business as a successful manager. It leads an individual to resist change and stay in personal old ways which prevent uncertain new approaches to solve life situations.

In business, Fear limits an individual's vision to see what lies beyond failures or errors.

The individual will be afraid of the consequences around trials than the actual price of what could be gained if succeed.

When fear possesses an individual, one chooses to stay the same, perceiving that trying to change will change him too, since change demands new skills, information and behaviours. …as Peter Senge once said, "people don't resist change, they fear being changed".

So when a being feel pushed to change in a situation, the way he views and understands the influences around him becomes narrow and self-centered. This feeling reduces an individual's ability to adapt to new upcoming situations which demand new information and skills.

In this psychology, an individual chooses to remain the same since his mind reminds him of the worst-case scenario if he chooses the unknowns. This mentality creates the behaviour within an individual to do the same thing at work or in life which might have failed before just because he is afraid to change.

So, an individual fears that if he chooses to change for the change, then he becomes the victim of change, and might fail since he is moving in the direction of the unknown. The unknown might demand from an individual to plan and set technologically advanced goals, or maybe coming up with new ways which might have never been done before in the industry.

In the unknown, there are demands which might change an individual's management styles and psychology around the ways which he normally operates, igniting fear in an individual to perceive his importance as being reduced.

> When an individual fears the unknown, you will hear one asking questions like ''what will be lost if I do this?'' instead of asking, ''what can I gain from this action?''.

Fear reduces an individual's perspective, so in order for a being to grow than fear's influences, one should learn intra-personal skills, by asking thyself positive questions about possibilities around personal growth rather than resisting change. If a person resists change in life and at work, then it is important to understand that "the opposite of growth is death", death in an individual career.

> Resisting change is death because remaining constant while the world is moving forward makes a constant being to be left behind and, in the future, those outdated skills and information become irreverent, and unproductive for a business's success.

Lacking **focus** on certain executions due to the changing stimuli in business and personal life makes an individual fail since this withdraws persistence, delaying completion of targeted plans and goals. This happens as the environment might confront an individual with difficult unpredicted challenges and newly presented information. The information which might show an individual that some of his preconceptions were wrong, about how to achieve those targeted plans.

So in business, the manager who desires growth should focus on great strategies and tactics to achieve targeted goals, accompanied by great executions even during times of change.

…thus, "if a plan fails to work, you have to work on the plan that is not going according to the plan".

Around this! an individual understands that if a plan fails to work towards desired goals, there should be another substituting plan to reach that goal.

…that's when we need focus, to truly maximise the chances of each tried plan to succeed. So below I am going to show you some focusing strategies which you can use to work on in your business.

An individual can keep up his focus around a plan by formulating timing strategies, these timing strategies answer,

(6) What?

(7) How?

(8) and When? questions

So, if the executed plan is not performing well, the plan setter needs to come up with answers to the question of **"What?"**, asking oneself and his team, **what is the problem?** or **what needs to be substituted?**.

This timing strategy helps an individual to keep the focus on the goal and coming up with new solutions to the identified problem.

An individual will grow to understand that some of the plans might have been overestimated in an underestimated situation. This might led the plan into failure but keeping the focus on the plan gives an individual room for improvement, coming up with new ideas on other substitute plans to approach the targeted goal.

...keep in mind that it's not about abandoning plan A, but rather focusing on it till you see if there is any fruit in it.

So, this question of what? is examined focusing on the areas which are failing, and developing an understanding of the causes of that problem.

After you are aware of the causes of the problem, you will know what to do to solve that problem. For example, in business the manager might notice a decrease in sales of a product which is anticipated to be successful in the future, then after doing some research on the cause of falling sales, he can find out that there is stiff competition in the market which is leading the product to fail in sales.

....we have identified the problem (stiff competition) by asking what? what is causing a decrease in sales?.

Then a growing manager can keep up individual focus in these timing strategies by answering the question, **"How?"**.

Coming up with ideas around **how to solve the problem?**...in this case (stiff competition).

Since you developed the awareness on what the problem is, and how it started,...(decrease in sales caused by stiff competition).

If the goal is to increase sales of this new product but sales are heading the opposite way due to charging high prices in a competitive market.

(How to solve the problem?)...You can implement new reduced pricing to the existing price so that customers increase demand on the product, perceiving it to be of the same value after the price decrease.

In this perception, if you substitute the existing plan without further visiting how? the question, you might lose customers and fail as a competent manager by solving the problem in the wrong way.

For instance, if you substitute your pricing, customers might perceive the product as of low value than the competitors, and then choose your competitor's products again. So, customers in this scenario should perceive the product to be of the same value even after the new low price, and the question you should ask now is "how?"

Well, in the timing strategies, the most fundamental question to know is "when?", in order to do your "how?". You should keep your focus on how to do things at the right time.

So, the question "when?" comes if you want to apply a new strategy, developing awareness on the right time to implement that strategy, while removing the old one successfully. For example, you identified that the problem to falling sales is stiff competition in the market!, after identifying how to solve this problem (charging lower prices than competitors), you should know when to implement the assumed solution (these cancelled prices with new lower below on the same price tag during holidays and promotions)…winning more customers through scramble buys.

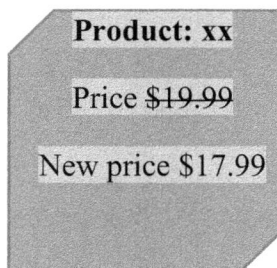

Product: xx

Price $~~$19.99~~

New price $17.99

CHAPTER 4

THE TIGER: "You can only fight the way you practice"…(Miyatomo Musashi)

The own boss

These are highly capable intelligent individuals who are street smart and have great independence of thoughts.

Psychology of the Tiger

Individuals with this psychology value independence and desire to do things themselves with a steady of thought. They hate to be told what to do, so they start their businesses with control over everything in the way they desire. In this psychology, a being has a burning ambition to do great things on his own and is ready for the next big thing to come in life. The Tiger prepares new information from friends, business connections, and the internet to enhance knowledge capacity to be able to view business from a bigger perspective.

In business, the Tiger is aware of what people want and has it in mind to sell an idea which he perceives to benefit others, at the same time making money and profits. This mentality engages the Tiger into different types of research and developments which consist of comparing different backgrounds about information towards the business of interest.

This mindset helps the Tiger to believe in himself as a talented being who is capable of success in life and work. His bravery is tapped by a strong positive mindset, faith and commitment to conquer personal fears around failure.

In this psychology, an individual also believes that "life is what you make it" meaning -" the daily habits you choose determine your future". This belief helps an individual to be aware of his actions, determining if he is progressing or regressing around targeted goals.

The tiger keeps personal motivation up at consistency as he desires to survive in all outcomes and is prepared for the worst, expecting the best in every situation. This psychology leads the Tiger to practice street smart moves through trials and errors, and gain experience when fail. He then comes up with improved surviving strategies in those failed situations or when noticing other people fail before him.

In this psychology, the Tiger is a hard worker who understands that money doesn't fall from trees like leaves, and to get it you have to create plans and work for its possession. In this mindset, his spiritual perceptions are elevated to believe that God helps people who help themselves -" so you have to be smart and be aware".

If the Tiger starts a business, he desires to catch all the opportunities presented to him with the belief that... "YOU CAN BE IN IT, TO WIN IT". He prepares himself to be the best at what he does, meeting up with time and placing himself in the face of opportunities. This personal placement is triggered by an individual's belief that the deal is halfway done if you just show up at the right time.

Wooden Allen once said, *"eighty percent of success is showing up"*.

Spiritual perceptions

Personal beliefs being parallel to work identity

(Genesis 35:11)..."I am God Almighty, be fruitful and increase in number. A nation and a community of nations will come from you, and kings will come from your body..."

In this perception, an individual has a difficulty in maintaining his personal beliefs because the ability to keep spirituality intact is parallel to his work identity. He might believe that God is existing in his life and to everyone but the talents he possesses will tempt him to consider himself as God.

The Tiger is a very talented being who can excel from the ground to become valuable around situations in which he used to be invisible. His abilities grew him to believe that he possesses the ability of the gods, and in this psychology, he can however vex himself by forgetting the source of his creation.

For example in this case let's use a professional doctor, "When a patient who is on comma rushed into the hospital, the doctor's skills are demanded to determine the death and life of the other human being. These responsibilities lead him to questions the existence of the creator God by formulating questions like,

"Does God choose to take others while letting others live?", or

"Do l possess powers to choose who to save or not?" and,

"Why is he this?, Why is he that?"

He gets puzzled from time to time with his work identity towards spirituality and in order to understand and grow, he should know that God did gave him the ability to become a god in his image and when someone is needing help, it is his responsibility to help the person at his best. Some patients might die, some might survive and the reason is only known by the creator God, we call this fate.

So when a situation is demanding the ability to make people happy, healed, motivated, educated, enlightened, and so on, it is up to us to perform at our full potential and let nature do the rest.

So, performing talents at best having in mind that, the use of these abilities with arrogance and self-worship thoughts will lead to the doom of an individual like Lucifer the musician's fate in heaven, is wisdom.

God helps people who help themselves

(Ecclesiastes 9:10)..."Whatever your hand finds to do, do it with all your might, for in the grave, where you are going, there is neither working nor planning nor knowledge nor wisdom."

In this perception, the Tiger knows to some extent the power he possesses when it comes to determining his future. He understands that people do not decide their future but they choose habits and these habits choose one's future. This understanding makes him very careful being who is aware of his actions.

The tiger perceives that if he sleeps, he will be left out since other people are competing for the same dream, and is motivated by his passion to work tirelessly to achieve his targeted goals. In order to reach his goals, he performs at his full potential, while giving himself some extra time in training for new skills around his abilities.

So, in this perception, If an individual finds himself in an upside-down situation, he perceives that it is up to him to think smart and turn the situation right-side up.

Success takes a leap of faith

(Ecclesiastes 9: 11)....the race is not to the swift or the battle to the strong, nor does food come to the wise or wealth to the brilliant or favour to the learned, but time and chance happen to them all.

Individuals with this perception put effort and wait with faith for the opportunity to represent its-self. When they see an opportunity they jump in to perform at their best potential, and If the individual's effort fails to work, one tries again and again till there is a breakthrough. Being aware that it might seem difficult at first to challenge one's talents to reach new heights but, as the individual continues to train thyself to perform at personal best, the goal will be reached.

In this perception, an individual's faith helps the mind to believe that he is a super-human being, an individual who can make anything possible as long as he imagines it possible. Faith grows an individual's spiritual perceptions to accept more challenging situations which might require more patience and specialized skills for progress.

Financial perceptions

Unpredictable income

In this financial perception, an individual perceives that "you earn what you earn", meaning there is no assurance of a fixed amount of money coming in as salary and compensation. An individual's monthly income fluctuates, giving the dependency to his earning each month, depending on what he offers to his clients.

The financial life of the Tiger is very unpredictable, unlike an employee who has a fixed income every month. Understanding this develops the eagerness to produce the best product that sells its-self, which customers will love and draws satisfaction.

The individual's unpredictable income leads to the development of personal appraising, and the ability to compete in the changing technological era. Developing awareness that rivals also desire to increase their shares in the market and it's up to me to make products which stand above the competition.

Educational Perceptions

Control your education

In this perception, an individual perceives oneself as the boss of his education with assistance from home, work, and friends. He understands that as individuals we choose what we want to attend, and how to organise that information to become us. Attending information with awareness screening any information that does not lead to a better person in the individual expertise.

With this perception, an individual's goal is to become the best at what he does, and personal attention is very reserved around those interests. This reserved attention improves an individual's ability to weigh education or information to see if it fits, or not in the pursued career. So, an individual is aware that he needs to choose the best ideas which suit personal talents and interests.

Other individuals may suggest different ways to do things for him to grow, but he knows himself better, with desires to grow what he already has in different ways, by keeping his best performance up with professional demands.

In business, after setting a goal, an individual with this perception gathers all information that is necessary around personal interests, and then organise that information to see which ideas are best to implement. This psychology is supplemented by the ability to interpret and make connections between pieces of information perceived as relevant in the career.

Well, an individual with this perception needs to learn new skills and update personal abilities frequently, being aware of the relevance of learning around the dynamic business industry.

Seek information to expertise

In this perception an individual values to learn new self-developing skills till one become an expert in a particular profession. An individual might have reached tertiary levels in education and or self-educated thyself about a certain type of business of interest, till absorbing the concept to produce great results. So, an individual produces great results due to repetitive training, spending more time seeking information, and practising how to perform better from personal previous outcomes.

As one continues with repeating the practise, it develops a technique of how to perform a certain skill till it becomes the way one fights challenges. Being aware that for an individual to be the best in the expertise, one is supposed to work on what he is already good at, in different ways.

So, for this to be effective in life and business, the individual needs to neutralize what he sucks at, by assigning it to others who can perform better and then expertise around personal talents.

In business, an individual with this perception desires expertise because of the awareness that clients retention is based on how well one did to the client or other clients before. So if a quality product/service is provided to a customer, it will advertise its-self to other individuals, creating a growing reach around potentially interested clients. In this awareness, the Tiger is demanded to provide satisfying quality products/services to a client at hand for more clients in the future.

Learn from your mistakes

The Tiger being, understands that an individual can fail in life due to trial and error of personal plans. To avoid more errors, when making a plan to do something, he weighs his opportunities and threats, because he knows that life can throwback punches at him as reality. As Mike Tyson once said, "we all have a plan till we get punched in the face".

So as an individual when you decide to plan something, you should be able to take a punch from reality and keep moving by punching back with extra strength.

A growing own boss might have faced some setbacks which led some of his ideas to fail, but he got smarter from those experiences and learned from his own mistakes. Experience gives an individual awareness around what is demanded from him in the next chance after a failure,....which is an improved approach. If for example, you failed before because you were operating solo, you can approach your business differently by hiring the right people around you, on which you can outsource some of your business tasks.

However, you should know how to hire the right people, the right people who can stand with you towards the achievement of your goals even if you change your plans and approaches. For example, a professional doctor might decide to research on, *"how to cure pain?"* In his team, If he has people who are willing to come up with the best painkiller, they can even change their direction after discovering that their found painkiller has side effects on the patient. So, this change can happen since the right people will be willing to change their plans and perceptions, as long as it is getting them closer to cure pain (without side effects). And mistakes can be learned to become a new experience when performing the search again for improvement. This experience is gained when the hired team choose to weigh factors that led to past failures to substitute them with new improved approaches.

…Henry Ford once said "Failure is simply the opportunity to try again…", and this time with experience and grown intelligence.

Relationship perceptions

I could not go through this chapter without touching on what the professional and own boss business beings perceive about relationships, relationships affect an individual greatly towards the growth of one's business and career.

Do relationships need extra time?

The Tiger perceives that a relationship needs its own time apart from work, and is aware of other family sacrifices which come wrapped around with it. With this perception, an individual is afraid to commit to a relationship believing that the time demanded to grow a business, might be equal to the time demanded to grow a family.

So, understanding that for a relationship to grow, it needs to be attended to, the Tiger may not have in mind the plan to substitute personal business of interests for relationships. Believing that sacrifices that are demanded by a relationship can steal one's time, time to get new deals and to create something new for business growth.

Besides the individual's unwillingness to commit to a relationship, the tiger is very charming when it comes to attracting the opposite sex, but most of the individual's intentions are not settle. So in this perception, an individual normally develops a relationship to see a partner on stressing and free times. This is because the individual might be too busy to settle with others to devote time which substitutes work interests.

…will discuss the importance of relationships as we go through this chapter.

Small loyal circle

The Tiger's circle is very small, he chooses to associate with people who he can benefit from and exchange. Connecting with other people who are doing business in his interests and grow with them, developing loyalty within their circle.

Their business relationships are very strong and they understand each other deeply like a bonded family. These bonds are created through loyalty which might have been shown in past experiences. One might have been in situations looking for help and approached others, and got that help from the ones who encourage the individual's growth. This further creates connections to help each other out, developing a more strong circle of supporting loyal friends.

This small circle keeps an individual up to date with the changes in the market and anything which might lead to loss of profit in the future. Also exchanging resources to cover for each other in times of need, and may have survived before using this strategy.

Don't trust people

An individual with this perception believes that "the society is a dog eating dog", and does not trust people. He believes that other people's interests are self-centered, and when given a chance to get what they want, an individual can rarely think of others. The tiger might have been in that business relationship or noticed other people serving their interests by letting others down.

In this perception, an individual always thinks about what could go wrong after developing a close relationship with other individuals.

If one gets in a business with people, he is suspicious of their interests expecting to see the worst possible outcome for doing business with the other party.

For instance, some of the wealthy business people when they are involved in small businesses owned by Tigers, their goal is to gain control of the business and then kick the owners out of their own business. Victimised Tigers at first might have thought that it was a deal for which both parties will benefit but as time goes on, they noticed it to be the vultures meat.

This experience gives the Tiger awareness to be alerted when people get too close, and create a rule that even when a situation gets tough, the other party's hand is risky. However for an individual to grow in this perception he needs to understand how to negotiate, the terms and conditions of a deal, and the creation of boundaries that protect one's business.

....will discuss negotiations further in the next chapter.

....

What it takes to be the Tiger

Let's go short and precise,...

Bravery

An individual has to be brave to be considered the Tiger. Because in this perception when an individual starts a business, it is usually from the ground, and the business has no guaranteed finance from the external sources.

In this scenario many people might tell the tiger that, what he wants is out of reach, providing all sorts of reasons to show how the idea might not work. These views can be touching and frightening for the individual, but bravery will give the power to understand that, every individual has the power to create his destination.

...." *if you are not fighting to win, you are fighting to lose"*.

In this psychology an individual can re-think the success of his intentions, also weighing the relevance of other people's views, but is demanded to choose for thyself between the comparison in the future or staying the same. So, for a person to develop awareness around making stupid choices perceiving them to be brave, he should examine the difference between constructive criticism from negativity, and develop the willingness to take the next steps without fear.

Walter Bagehot said, *"the great pleasure in life is doing what people say you cannot do."*

Setting unique challenges

The tiger needs to think ahead of his current situation to come up with solutions in challenging situations. Thinking ahead leads a being to be creative and lift a person from his comfort zone. As one thinks ahead, vision is developed within to picture the future in life and business with ideas on how to get there.

An individual can set challenges in form of objectives that needs to be accomplished in a specific period. These challenges will be one's road map towards the bigger picture even if there are distractions in the way.

Challenges can be tough and sometimes the body can be lazy to follow up, but a well-written goal can lift a being off his butt and make a person work hard, to feel fulfilled around the written obligation. If a person does not work to achieve these unique goals, he will feel unfulfilled, losing, and unhappy since the sense of completeness comes from meeting one's goals.

Well, for a being to accomplish targeted goals in life, realistic plans should be set, and be willing to follow the discipline of each selected plan.

Discipline

In this perception, an individual has to be very disciplined since there is no boss who breaths down on one's neck to remind, "hey dude! you are supposed to do this".

The own boss is his source of motivation around life and business challenges, though losing motivation does happen from time to time. An individual can lose motivation from failures, distractions, and other negativity from the external environment. However, the real Tiger picks thyself up and revisits the thoughts that made eagerness to start to continue the journey towards success.

In this growth, after an individual starts the journey, the journey might seem uncertain in the future, and thinking only about that can be energy draining. So one has to remember that, when 1 started the journey, the future was uncertain and so is now, but instead 1 chose to prepare for the future because 1 want something better.

This bravery perception instils discipline in an individual to know what to do and what not to do as long as the end goal is in the mind.

However, if the to-do list is too much, the individual can overwork himself and feel tired from too much work, diminishing potential creativity.

Overworking may happen when the individual feels like unable to walk away from work even if wanting to since sometimes the objective at hand is demanded by customers in time and should be provided at high quality.

So in this discipline, an individual should resolve overworking by scheduling some time off in these plans and follow that discipline to keep personal energy recharged.

Switch off time

The Tiger should arrange a switch-off time to be away from work and have time with family to watch some movie or out for lunch. Switch off time improves social life and personal development by refreshing as one communicates with others.

Switch off time can help an individual to discover what's happening in life, on the other hand continuing plans with newly developed ideas to work on in the future.

As an individual works in this perception, awareness grows to understand that my counterparts and family may need me to be present for some of their important life events. And my presents can help to strengthen relationship ties with people around me, giving reasons to other people to stand by me in my times of need.

However, undisciplined switch-off times can lead an individual to give oneself more time to personal life than business's interest. So what should we do?

The tiger is supposed to come up with some strict working patterns which can get him lonely at times, and create necessary strict switch-off times. These strict patterns can help an individual to stay disciplined when it's time to work, also following personal switch-off times.

Handling loneliness

Since there is no manager to assist an individual to get through tough times, or a supervisor with some years of experience and wisdom to guide here, you are on your own.

This scenario isolates you, creating a feeling of being separated from other people. In this perception, an individual will discover that "I have a lot of responsibilities, and spending most of my time with others might not hand me over my goals, so l have to develop the will to be alone as l work for my dreams".

Most individuals don't grow from this perception because their mind tells them that it is boring to be alone(the sheep psychology). So they end up going back into the groups and forget their goals, beginning to be consumed by new interests and influences. However, when an individual fails to handle loneliness, one can delay personal targeted goals and miss opportunities in life and business.

This delay can cause an individual to be miserable since one knows that, I am living undesired life due to my failure to handle loneliness.

So, for an individual to successfully handle loneliness, one should be encouraged to be bored for future happiness after achieving. While trying to avoid complete loneliness by creating networks that build connections with other people who are similar in life.

. . . .

The Drowning Tiger

As l continued with the journey to unleash the tiger being, I discovered 3 factors that all experienced own bosses agreed to must have been drowning their careers as they start to put their ideas into existence.

Lack of capital

The tiger has limited access to capital from large institutes and banks for business start-ups and growth. This individual normally seeks funding to venture into a business from friends, and limited loans from the bank, which may not be enough to buy enough machinery and other resources. So, this factor alone is enough to limit one's growth into a successful business owner, since some life-changing ideas may not be sponsored to become a reality.

Lacking machinery

When an individual starts a company, the resources to do work effectively at a faster rate will be expensive to afford. So, the business can produce small units to meet niche customer's needs at a very low rate in supply.

The slow rate in supplying might be a result of the amount of time being taken by production processes to finish each unit. On the other hand, the individual's machinery might be second hand and primitive to work effectively, requiring constant repairs which then delays production processes to meet customer demands, leading business to serve a small market from potential customers.

This factor limits business growth since customers who might need services now are not being well served, these customers might then decide to buy the same provisions from the business's competitors. So as customers keep on switching from another service provider when there are not well served, the business's customer retention becomes more unpredictable since customers are losing loyalty.

Financial illiteracy

The Tiger can face difficulty in understanding financial management when starting a business, and this factor can also limit growth due to loss of money that is not being used at its full capacity in the business operations.

This financial illiteracy sometimes leads the business into losses, For example, an individual might decide to make sales on products while giving away discounts not well calculated in order to gain and keep more customers in the future. However, this unawareness of business finances can lead to huge losses which may result in the closure of the business.

This financial illiteracy is normally caused by the desire to start a business without seeking financial knowledge to increase financial returns around that business. Then when an individual decides to start a business, the financial management can slip his claws, resulting in being drowned by large debts and losses.

Well, an individual can gain these skills as experience continues to grow while seeking more knowledge from business mentors or coaches, as discussed further below on the growth of the tiger's career.

So, for an individual to keep growing around this factor, there is a need to learn how to spread personal wings in all areas of the business from financial management to other departments.

....

Growth of the Tiger's career

If an individual has what it takes to be the own boss, there is also a need to continuously grow into more than being an ordinary own boss to escape drowning. Imagine this being growing some wings on the back, Ya! a flying being with enhanced abilities from the ones which are already possessed.

Thinking outside the box

An individual who is capable of thinking outside the box is very creative in solving life and business problems. In this psychology, there is no barrier to move forward or seeing new possibilities. One will be able to see a problem and find ways to solve it uniquely, for example like a business person coming up with ways to introduce a new product that is different from one in the market x10.

In business, an individual should challenge his mind to reach some creative states to brainstorm some ideas to be weighed for performance. Brainstorming allows a person to develop choices to choose from while growing unlimited idea generation.

As an individual continues to be creative, creative ideas gain momentum in coming up with solutions easily, then solve more life problems.

However, for an individual who is in this growth to be successful, there is a need to push oneself to always stay creative in any difficult life situation.

Remember! there is no one to tell you when to do so.

Seeking mentors and coaches

A growing boss understands that mindset needs to be groomed, to perceive situations with knowledge and wisdom. In this growth, an individual seek mentors from people who are doing best in the business of interest, and is willing to attend to their ideas, shared experiences, and discipline. This helps them to walk in a better-improved path which is revised from their own experiences. So, a wise boss is also aware that in order to grow successfully, l need different mentors with different talents and experiences on different business aspects, so that l can use that knowledge to solve each different scenario presented in life.

Since an individual within this growth has no manager to report to, coaching also helps to grow in business. Coaching helps with guidance, and how to react in situations just like an experienced individual, growing from being an amateur. However, before approaching a potential mentor or any help, an individual should know the person to whom is approaching, and how that person is supposed to help.

Seeking mentor,

State exactly what you want?

    how you want it?

when you want it?

    how the people around you might help?

and how this person can help you before involving them?

"Stating exactly what you want, will help you to see the bigger picture of that desire, also developing awareness in mind on the exact way you may want that desire to happen…."

…..'' you have to know the exact time which you want that desire to happen while weighing around in the environment to see if there is anyone who can help you to reach those desires, and then choose a mentor/coach who is capable of helping you to reach those particular desires."

If you become aware of how to seek a mentor or coach, you will choose the right ones in a specific situation, measuring the progress of your journey as connected to that mentor, while examining if you are still on track with your goals.

Willingness to delegate

Being the own boss and trusting people to do tasks on one's behalf is very difficult. In this perception, an individual is not willing to delegate tasks to other people. This is triggered by the belief that no one can perform my work as l do. The own boss's skills are very unique, and the replication of presented talents may only be performed by himself in a similar situation.

However, the growing Tiger needs to understand that, in order to grow, a person should delegate some tasks to other people who might possess talents in thy weakness, with the awareness on when to delegate? how to delegate? and to whom before involving the other person.

….**let me answer this short and simple.**

Delegation is vital for business growth because as the business grows, its roles become more difficult to be performed heterogeneously. This situation demands a growing individual to develop a willingness in outsourcing some tasks which are not his strong unit into better hands. **The hands which can help you to work at ease, as you stay in your genius zone**, keeping the focus on tasks which you truly love to perform.

You might want to read that again to stick it in.

The right people around your business

An individual with the tiger's perceptions needs to understand that **"no one man can surround the hill"**. This awareness can help to make important partners around work, products and markets with people who can support business growth. These partners should have business goals aligned with yours, in other words, you should both want to create the same thing. These partnerships should go beyond the desire to grow money but rather having the same idea on how the business suppose to look like in the future. Some of these partners are also reliable and can support the business's identity and interests by providing some capital and ideas in difficult times.

Bear in mind that, as business individuals make partnerships, they should be clear to each other on how to work in the future around their partnership agreement. This clarity reduces the consequences that may arise if one individual is involved in a partnership or agreement without verifying the deal. (Jacob's story in the next chapter).

Note. if an individual refuses to partner up with important business individuals, the business's survival can be at risk in terms of how to win since it is a team of one man.

Chapter 5

THE EAGLE: "where there is no vision, people perish"…(bible wisdom)

The Leader

This is a committed individual who leads others by stimulating higher performance standards, in pursuing a clear and compelling vision.

Beliefs of the Eagle

A leader believes that "where there is no vision, people perish", meaning when individuals do not know where they are going, they probably lose self-control. This awareness gives the leader know-how of the need around showing people a clear picture of exactly where they are going. He believes that, if the one who is leading does not know where he is leading people, the leader and his followers will head for failure.

This belief also develops the awareness that "The blind cannot lead the blind". So, for anything to advance or develops in business and life, it requires a visionary leader. A leader who sees the future beyond the limitations of any negative influence and uncertainty. Leaders with long enhanced vision are being demanded in this modern generation, who possess the ability to ask themselves and others questions about the future.

This psychology helps the leader to figure out where he is going, and how to get there while putting aside everything that can steal that dream. With this perception, an individual can see the other side of an outcome believing in taking risks to accomplish. Knowing that "nothing comes to you unless you take risks in life, and work hard for what it is that you are visioning". Around this risk-taking belief, an individual grows to understand the demands of the journey before jumping in.

In business, the leader believes that "when you have a bigger dream, the challenges, the struggle, the journey and the level of commitment becomes bigger". Developing an enhanced vision to see opportunities and threats ahead, and the willingness to show others what is being faced to come up with better ways on how to prepare for the future.

At work, the leader also believes that his workers are **theory Y** type from Douglas McGregor's perceptions, and perceive that workers around him like work, and are committed individuals who have ambitions around their lives. So when challenges come in business, the leader believes that his employees will enjoy these challenges with eagerness to win. This perception further helps the leader to know who to involve in his crucial business events by assigning sensitive tasks to more responsible individuals.

Values and desires

In this psychology, a being desires to lift people in their perceptions around spirituality, finance, education, relationships and other life-related aspects. At work, the leader can help others through training so as to develop them by his guidance on how to bring the best out of themselves as he can. This happens because the leader values productivity and progressing from those who are around, being aware of individual's results, appreciating them from the smallest perceived task understanding that, "small things matter because they are the beauty in helping to build the bigger goal".

Mostly, a leader values the transformation of information that is possessed by an individual into productivity. The leader values productivity to the extent of breaking traditions in life if those traditions can stop full potential towards reaching desired goals.

Educational perceptions

Improving knowledge

The eagle is a very talented individual who has reached talents extensions through seeking knowledge and working hard. Through the learning process, he became aware of the dynamics around the technological era and has developed the ability to see what might change on which he can meet with personal skills. These skills to lead a business and people are taught by great leaders and intelligent individual's who possess more information than him, with the willingness to teach others the information to stick it further in mind.

As mentioned earlier on desires, when an individual with this perception learns new information and skills, his main motive is to also teach others to master those new skills and information to become better.

So, knowledge-seeking in this perception enhances individual wisdom to see situations differently, developing an ability to analyse the future to come up with predictions that might make better choices.

Predicting the future

Predicting the future is one of the most important areas to grow in leadership, by learning how to visualise it as if it is present. This visualisation helps the leader to see the future beyond where he wants to be, also seeking to understand what it takes to be at that particular desired future. This vision gives an individual the exact picture of what he wants while knowing how to get it.

In this journey, one might face predicted and unpredicted setbacks which might try to stop targeted goals, however, the leader is ready to overcome these threats with opportunities.

So in this perception, an individual develops awareness on how to predict the future by reading books and or life experiences that might be noticed in the past around a reoccurring situation.

Bonus: Learning how to negotiate

As promised in the previous chapter,

An individual should seek to understand the other side of a business agreement that is intended to be negotiated. This is done by verifying the other party's intentions on that particular deal before an agreement.

When you become aware of what the other party wants, you can develop a strategy that taps into the other party's driving emotions, a strategy that can give others what they want while getting what you want (win-win situation).

To make the negotiation clear, an individual can ask questions to the other party around areas which he seeks to understand. Also reading carefully before signing the terms and conditions of a negotiation to see if what you want is written in the exact expected way.

If the other party's interests are not meeting your line of expectations, you can negotiate the deal again. This requires an individual to possess skills on how to acknowledge what the other party wants, to get help from them on meeting the line of expectation around that negotiation.

However, if an individual does not understand the terms and conditions of a negotiation, consequences can be costly to the way one lives and around future business operations.

A typical unverified negotiation

Jacob's story

In the Jewish bible, in Genesis 29, Jacob met his uncle Laban, his mother's brother in search of a wife as his father Isaac had advised him. When Jacob got into the house of Laban, Laban asked Jacob his willing compensation in return for the labour he provided. Since Jacob was in love with Rachael, the second daughter of Laban after Leah, he suggested working seven years for her hand in marriage. In Laban's customs, the second daughter was not supposed to be married before the first daughter. Thus, Jacob did not verify these terms and conditions on his agreement to work for seven years. When Jacob finished his agreed seven years for a wife, he was tricked into sleep with Leah. Jacob then got angry and tried to explain their agreement but Laban defended himself with the marriage custom on which Jacob did not verify during their bridal negotiation.

In this story, Jacob should have verified his deal to marry Rachael after seven years. When Laban saw that Jacob was not aware of the customs, he used those customs against him and made him work for another seven years for Rachael, who was supposed to be married before Leah in the first seven years.

When an individual is unable to negotiate or fails to verify the negotiation, the consequences can lead to costly life and or exploitation by the other party. So, in this educational perception, the leader should learn how to negotiate,- thinking fast in verifying the terms and conditions of a deal.

Financial Perceptions

Planning risks

In this financial perception, an individual should understand the importance of developing new skills to manage risks. These new skills to manage risks will help you to make less risky decisions in your personal life and business, since you plan for your risk management.

Planning can also help you to reduce uncertainty and avoid risky decisions in business. With this awareness, the leader can navigate changing landscape around the perceived financial future, and be able to update the plan to fit in those changing situations.

So this anticipation of the future events - good or bad, leads an individual to think in advance and how to respond to those events. Developing the room for thyself, which helps to avoid being hurried into decisions when faced with unexpected events.

Planning risks can help an individual to check if he is working around important financial issues and to check if anything is overlooked. This helps to develop a behaviour that is aligned with good risk management in the business at hand.

However, with this awareness, financial planning should not be viewed in isolation, but rather in context with every aspect of an individual's business and personal life as a leader.

Taking risks

A leader in this perception when finally choose to take a risk can put more personal time in learning choices of investments then invest money to grow. The leader is aware of what can happen if an individual takes on a risk without having enough information around that investment. Thus, if an individual jumps into an investment without knowledge, is likely to lose everything in that risky approach. This develops an individual's know-how around the difference between a risk and a risky approach. Enabling the individual to take risks wisely by weighing the important knowledge that is required to gain financial return around chosen risk.

However, when an individual reaches personal limitations around financial perceptions in taking risks, one should associate thyself with other individuals who possess more financial skills than thy in that particular area for help.

So in short, taking a risk is knowing what you know, and what you don't know around a particular investment option. Developing awareness that encourages you to take risks, knowing that to grow money I have to put it where knowledge and experience reside.

Increasing sales and profit

The goal of every financial leader in business is to cut costs and increase the profit margin on products/services which are being sold to customers. In this perception, an individual creates products at a maximum low cost of production while offering high quality around that product.

The aim from this perspective is to increase profit at anything that business does while satisfying the targeted customers for retention. So when an individual with this perception produces a product in the market, the aim is to grow by increasing sales of what is being produced.

Sales can be increased by making developments on the product/service to be more customer-friendly and, or serve customer complaints while fighting to be ahead of competitors in the dynamic technological industry. This then allows an individual to stay profitable in business, and if possible staying around on top with the most selling-successful growing businesses in that industry.

Spiritual Perceptions

Growing spirituality

(1 Peter 2:2)...Like newborn babies, crave pure spiritual milk, so that by it you may grow up in your salvation,

The leader understands the importance of spirituality as a life-changing ground. He desires to grow more in spirituality through meditations, praying and attending spiritual programs constantly. With this perception, the individual is aware of the death of his spirituality if it is not growing, and if the individual's spirituality is falling, it will be difficult for the person to overcome procrastination, demotivations and quitting. These states can be influenced or influence an individual to lose vision, faith and patience while trapping the individual under repeated behaviours that delay targeted goals.

The fall in spirituality can take down a leader back to the sheep, into a person who doubts and is unable to complete a started task after being trapped by these spiritual draining states. However, these spiritual downturns require the leader to quickly see that he is no longer himself, and consult some other people who might be on better ground to help to become himself once more. So, attending to these spiritual programs and positive psychology grows an individual's perceptions to be attracted by better stimuli that develop well-being as a leader.

Faith and patience

(Hebrews 6:12)"....We do not want you to become lazy, but to imitate those who through faith and patience inherit what has been promised."

In this perception the leader is connected to spirituality, to keep his faith and patience in every process of what he does. In these processes of achieving his vision, he sets high standards towards completion of each stage that can make him closer to his vision.

Having faith and patience helps an individual to understand that, "things do take time to accomplish, and to stay envisioned an individual should see his future situation as if it is being present at the moment".

On emphasis, this faith is kept intact as mentioned earlier by attending spiritual programs like meditation and positive psychology, why? to develop new ideas in an individual, even if the current situation appears bad. This then helps the individual to remain calm as he comes up with new ideas, blocking individual emotions to intervene in the process of creating and waiting.

The need to block emotions should come as soon as an individual process or starts something which might overrule one's intellectual self. However, when things turn the other side from an individual's expectations, one should continue working around set plans trying to get closer or accomplish the main objective. This demands more patience on the new plan and faith that the outcome will be successful.

....

What it takes to be the eagle

For a business to be successful it needs a leader, a leader who possesses vision beyond every obstacle, who can show others that vision, so as for them to live with it and work together to achieve that goal. Below, let's look at what it takes to be a leader who leads others and resources to develop a successful business,

Envision

The eagle has a vision about where he wants to go, and how to reach that desired destination. This vision is accompanied by acuity ability to focus on a clear picture of the exact thing he wants, and the exact results that must be achieved in the long run.

Envisioning takes place when a leader shares his vision with employees, to work together towards achieving that goal. When creating goals, a leader can ask thyself several questions about the future view from the present, visualising tomorrow before involving others. This quality also enhances the leader's ability to see the target from the present, and ways on how to snatch that target from now.

So in this vision, the leader should continue to envision also helping others to understand the desired bigger picture. In this awareness, a leader understands the importance of showing people where they are going, to best prepare themselves for future events.

Well, the leader should envision people and develop within them the eagerness to be competitive, then a stimulus to perform at full potential is ignited within them to reach set standards in pursuing the envisioned vision.

Strategic planning

The leader should understand the importance of strategic planning around a vision. When an individual possesses a vision of how the long term is supposed to look like, there is a need to also cater for the short term demands. So, the short-term view is the one step closer towards reaching long-term goals, this can develop awareness by formulating questions like, "what am I doing now for my survival as I am heading towards that long term vision"?

However, These short-term goals should not take the leader's vision away but rather help the leader to build a strong status quo along with long-term goals.

Note. Before formulating a strategy, the leader should assess the business and verify if his strategic planning can work with the organisational mission, vision and guiding principles. Then if the strategy is aligned, the leader can develop strategic goals, while communicating with employees on how they are going to work - then implement the set strategic planning.

As time moves, the leader should be able to track the status of the set strategy, analysing and evaluating the strategy -then communicate the progress with his helpers.

Showing integrity

Integrity - "is a state in which an individual possesses the ability to stay honest to oneself, following self-values while being ethical to others in the surrounding environment".

In this awareness, the leader knows that employees want to see the leader showing integrity in everything he does, to follow suit. This demands the leader to be completely true to oneself, and at work about what he said to be after. For others to follow his words, the true leader knows that he has to stand for his words otherwise the employees will not change since they always wait for him to change first.

So in this quality, when the leader says something that has to be worked for, he is demanded by his words and others to show the meaning through his actions. His followers expect to see him showing more effort and discipline in every aspect of doing business for them to understand what he meant.

However, the business can fail at some points and people can get annoyed by bad situations. These uncertainties require the leader to stay positive around his business goals while showing positive behaviours at work. Developing this quality gives the leader awareness that, to turn a bad situation around, a leader has to show sacrifices and sweat to improve the situation into reaching desired goals. ,

Well, if the leader shows integrity,- the morale, attitude, and level of commitment from people around him get transformed, bringing closer the success of targeted goals.

Empowering others

Empowerment is a transfer of power from the one who has more, the leader, to the one who has less, the subordinate (Forrester,2000), thus, empowering means granting power. In this quality, the leader seeks to make his followers independent at what they do by encouraging them and training them to be more effective in the dynamic business industry.

When the workers are demotivated and feel less competent in the organisation, the leader is demanded to present encouragement to his employees with new skills and new information on how to be competent.

In this quality, the leader desires to lift people and encourage independent thinking and decision-making from them in the organisation.

When employees are trained to perform certain tasks on their own, the leader should give them room to make mistakes and improve, by becoming more independent and confident. With this, the leader gives employees new challenges while supporting them to do even better next time. If an employee grows to become more skilled while possessing knowledge, trust may be developed between the leader and the employee, since this can ignite confidence within the leader to give an employee sensitive tasks at work. If an employee fails, the leader with this quality motivates employees because he is aware that 'motivations make people excited about what they are doing, and gives them strength to do better through pleasant and unpleasant situations'.

Ability to evaluate

In this ability, the leader is demanded to look at every quality which he is supposed to be, and growing willingness to evaluate his actions constantly. For this to be effective, the leader should understand that these qualities do not take one step after the other, but rather should be implemented together as long as the organisation exists. So when the leader envisions, develop strategic planning, show integrity, and empower others. During evaluation he is supposed to ask himself, "am 1 still being this?", if not why? and around people who work with him, he should be able to evaluate their progress along with the set measurement. If he finds them not progressing, he should ask again, "why is this not progressing?", and "what can 1 do or what can they do?", to improve into progress. In this quality, the leader is up-to-date with organisational progress, and is not difficult for him to measure results from that organisation's effort altogether.

Thus, evaluation helps the leader to find challenges that are associated with formulated questions and help him to find the exact answers which can draw him closer to his objectives,- continuing simultaneously to do what it takes to lead an organisation into success.

....

The difference:

(the eagle vs the elephant)-(The leader vs the manager)

✓ The manager has strength in tight control systems which monitor employee's activities constantly to avoid bottlenecks. He perceives that workers should be monitored because they don't like to work (theory X) by Douglas McGregor. These perceptions cause the manager to lose trust in employees thinking that they save their interests at work.

On the other hand, the leader believes he can hire the right people for the job and then trust them to do things on their own. He believes in (theory Y) type of employee who likes to work, an ambitious person like him in making the organisation and individual life a success.

✓ The manager focus on what needs to be done now and assign employees tasks they have to work on without much detail about future vision. This attribute leads to the completion of short-term objectives, though however, it leads the employees to feel unmotivated since they are not aware of the reason for their effort. So, in the employee's view, it is just checking in to do some monitored tasks then check out after.

The leader uses a paradox from Antoinne De Saint-Exupery which states that "if you want to build a ship, don't drum up people to collect the wood and don't assign them tasks and work, But rather teach them to long for the endless immensity of the sea". Thus, the leader shows his followers a bigger picture of what they are going to get through, and how to get through that situation.

This attribute in an organisation keeps employees alerted about the future challenges, understanding what they are supposed to do now and why they should do it. This awareness from the above saying gives employees the energy in preparing to withstand the situation by building a strong ship(a business).

✓ The manager views employees as individuals who just need to get paid to survive. In this view, the manager looks at employees as liabilities in the business, liability beings who can increase costs or losses if they are not properly utilised. This psychology is then observed by employees through management behaviour at work towards them. Leading employees to perceive themselves as not being part of the important team, since the manager is behaving in a way that makes them feel unimportant, like being just labour providers.

The leader makes this situation different by envisioning and empowering people who work with him towards business goals. He views employees as collaborators and assets to the business, employees who are there to help him in growing a successful business. These leadership qualities allow him to see everyone's contribution to the organisation in both pleasant and unpleasant situations. A leader then shows employees how important they are to the organisation by empowering them through initiating training programs, and then involve them in decision-making for more independent thinking.

✓ When there is a tradition in the business that is stopping progress to move from good to great, the leader breaks that tradition to enhance the business's productivity. This occurs since the leader can get frustrated by doing the same tasks which are not progressing at work, and is eager to come up with new ways of doing business from a different perspective.

However, The manager cannot afford to break tradition, his mind reminds him of what could go wrong asking himself "what if it doesn't go well?", or "what are the consequences of these actions?". These perspectives differentiate him more from the leader who sees the horizon of his actions by formulating questions like "what will we get from doing this?".

✓ The manager desires to maintain situations and follows traditions because it's the way he views things, viewing things as if he doesn't have the authority to call for some changes. So he then maintains things to make sure that everything is in the right place, and is done properly the way it is supposed to be, asking himself "what is not well?", if there is any, he puts things back to their exact position.

So, the leader comes into play and changes everything in ways which he sees fit around targeted goals while adapting to the business's future climate. This unique leadership behaviour differentiates him again from the manager being who follows a tradition of what has been happening, even if it can hinder the future growth of that organisation.

Note. Respect the difference, it's crucial for business survival.

It has been a question in the modern industries, "is the managerial leadership still relevant for the success of the organisation? or leaders should just focus on visionary leadership? This research had been conducted by thousand of leading researchers in the past and has been discovered that when a business focuses on managerial leadership only, it will erode since its focus on the future is limited but these leaderships should be balanced into strategic leadership. A leadership style that works with managerial leadership, and visionary leadership to accomplish current objectives while having in mind the long-term objective of the organisation.

....

The Fallen Eagles

: Why do successful leaders fall

Neglecting other people's opinions

Leadership is a powerful position, a position which can make an individual end up being obsessed with thyself to the extend of neglecting other people's opinions towards life solutions.

A leader can neglect other people's important opinions or facts when he feels challenged by those views and might develop the desire to show how powerful he is to others through arrogant actions. In this view, a leader can deny other individual's views and choose to continue doing what he sees fits, feeding his desire to just feel powerful around others.

The threat of feeling powerful is sometimes caused by employees or followers who grew to see life and business situations differently, while also growing the desire to do more in their careers, plus or other people who just enjoy challenging others. However, denying other people's opinions can make the threatened leader at work fail, this happens since the leader might be leading a business into the future which is not thoroughly prepared for or evaluated. This situation may end up in losses and organisational closures which can be difficult to compensate in the future.

Thus, for the leader to avoid this fall, he must understand that when people provide their opinions strongly, it is a window into their soul which needs the leader to attend and acknowledgement. So in this view, the leader can hear other individual's opinions, longings, fears, uncertainties and struggles before making his own choice.

This strategy can lead followers to give more valuable information in the future as they feel heard and seen as part of something on which they matter.

Overconfidence

Some leaders get overconfident in things they are doing and ignore the reality of the situation. In this view, it is not only about just do it mantra towards uncertain challenges but rather weighed ideas, assessed and evaluated plans towards the future.

If the leader has overconfidence at work, and however engages in the business's processes without giving conclusions from some real facts, he will fail. The leader should face facts that are being presented to him and should be able to choose how to just do it. In this scenario, maybe he needs help on extra resources, or maybe pulling away some of his resources in uncertain investments and, or stopping a certain operation as a whole. In these choices, the leader should bear in mind that he must never lose his business confidence, and must always stay self-aware around personal driving emotions in decision making. This checking on driving emotions around a certain choice can also be helped by other individuals around the leader, on which he can ask around for different views and minds to develop idea analysis.

Thus, these weighed ideas in confidence can enhance the leader's view by developing more awareness around the target, and other sides on which he didn't consider in his head.

Leadership fell due to overconfidence

The collapse of the Lehman brothers

Lehman Brothers had humble origins, tracing its roots to a general

108

store founded by German brothers Henry, Emanuel, and Mayer Lehman in Montgomery, Alabama, in 1844. After Henry died the other Lehman brothers expanded the scope of the business into commodities trading and brokerage services.

As the US economy grew into an international powerhouse, the firm prospered over the following decades and overcame plenty of challenges over the years. The company survived the railroad bankruptcies of the 1900s, the great depression of the 1930s, two world wars, a capital shortage when it was spun off by American Express (AXP) in 1994 in an initial public offering (IPO), and the Long Term Capital Management collapse and Russian debt default of 1998.

Despite its ability to survive past disasters, the collapse of the US housing market ultimately brought Lehman to its knees, since its headlong rush into the sub-prime mortgage market proved to be a disastrous step. After heading into the mortgage market, In the company's post-earnings conference call, Lehman's chief financial officer(Erin Callan) said the risks posed by rising home delinquencies were well contained and would have little impact on the firm's earnings. He also said, he did not foresee problems in the sub-prime market or hurting the economy.

After Erin's announcement Lehman stocks fell sharply as the credit crisis erupted in August 2007 disposing of their colossal miscalculation. The company started to close its business units and continued to suffer losses. Lehman CEO Richard Fuld's planned to keep the firm independent, by seeking support from other external sources but then failed, which made Lehman declared bankruptcy on September 12, 2008.

Overconfident leadership by the company's CEO's led the fourth-largest investment bank in the united states with 25, 000 employees worldwide to close with more liabilities than assets. It was a reminder to financial leaders and other leaders that when you approach the future you have to be prepared while being aware of your calculations and avoiding overconfidence by taking other people's views in times of uncertainty.

Trusting too much

In business and around a society trust is essential, since it builds confidence in others to assume them as possessing the quality of being trusted. When individuals want help from others, they seek people whom they trust, this trust then builds more confidence in other people as they continue helping, showing reliance in possessing the quality of being trusted.

This quality of being trusted in individuals and businesses contributed to the greatness of large organisations and great personalities around the world. Though however, when an individual trusts too much, he falls from where he is, especially in a leading position. So, when a leader has people or a team around him, who help around to achieve certain objectives, he should be aware of their personal goals and ambitions, since sometimes these people's hidden personal attributes can lead the leader into doom.

Thus, some individuals around the leader might want to take a position and possessions away from him, while leaving the leader in the ground with nothing. In my awareness, I call these jealous influences, hatred influences, and or greedy influences, knowing for sure that individuals who are possessed by these qualities, can take down the eagle above from the sky into the deep underground.

A leader who once fall by trusting too much

Case study

Steven Paul jobs was recognised as a pioneer of the personal computer revolution of the 1970s and 1980s, along with Apple co-founder Steve Wozniak. In 1985 he was forced out after a long power struggle with the company's board, and its then CEO John Sculley. John Sculley was recruited by Jobs himself with the now legendary pitch: *"do you want to sell sugared water for the rest of your life?, Or do you want to come with me and change the world?"*.At this point, Jobs wanted to be the CEO, but the board didn't think he was ready for it. The problem was that Steve Jobs had earned himself a reputation for being difficult to work with. Since he sweated the details often at the expense of his team's feelings and their deadlines. This came to a head in 1985 under Job's guidance when Apple had released the Lisa, the ever first computer with a graphical user interface (GUI). It was a technical marvel, but a total flop sales-wise. His follow-up project, the macintosh, sold better - but still not well enough to make a sizable dent in IBM's control of the PC market.

Sculley then moved to fire Jobs away from the macintosh product group, essentially putting reins on the founder and his influence at Apple. In response Jobs went straight to Apple's board of directors - who then sided with Sculley.

Steve Jobs was thrown out of his own company by underestimating his spheres, who then took that advantage and voted him out while he was still obsessed competing with Bill Gates about the new Macintosh idea. The idea which Jobs accused Gates of must have ripped off from his Macintosh computer after he trusted him to pre-look at it. Yet, on the other hand, Gates refused the accusation by saying "the main copying that went on relative to Steve Jobs and me is that we both benefited from the work that Xerox Parc did in creating graphical interface - it wasn't just them but they did the best work. Steve hired Bob Belville, I hired Charles Simonyi. We didn't violate any IP rights Xerox had, but their work showed the way that led to the Mac and Windows."

In the above case studies, Steve Jobs reviewed that he trusted Bill Gates, and trusted him as a partner to whom he then showed the macintosh idea. Gates as someone who wanted to create something big in the technological inventions, from this idea he found a way to create an advanced idea. When Microsoft released its first iteration of windows in 1985 back then, Jobs accused Gates of ripping off his idea when the two met in a conference room at Apple, where Jobs ripped into Gates, yelling "I trusted you, and now you're stealing from us!".

Getting tired

As human beings, we all get tired from time to time due to many different forces outside us, but as per our nature, we are rechargeable beings who can come back in form after that lost energy, from a little rest.

In this view, the leader is an individual who is expected by his followers and supporters to reach certain expectations in life and business. These expectations can be short-term, and or long-term objectives to be accomplished by the leader, which can however put pressure on the leader to the obligation. This pressure can be mounting when the leader fails to reach certain expectations which can also give chances to naysayers, and opposing parties to speak down against the leader on his competence. During this process, a leader can get tired and worse fail to focus clearly in the future. The future also holds unexpected life events, like the current Covid-19 pandemic which affected the whole world for a long period, leading many organisations into losses and closure. In these situations, some leaders can get tired of pursuing their long-term objectives, objectives that always require more energy, commitment and unwavering vision from them to be accomplished.

So, for the leader to avoid this fall and all other opposing forces, he should continue to seek knowledge, while being persistent in doing what it takes to be the Eagle.

Note, seek continuous spiritual guidance for self-alignment, - to generate even more strength and ideas around the business in this dynamic technological world.

P.s......" a great leader never lose patience"

Power obsession

As mentioned above, leadership is a powerful position, a position that can get an individual so obsessed by the power to the extent of refusing or unwilling to step down when he has to. In this behaviour an individual might perceive that if he leaves the leadership position, it might make him powerless and nothing important around his environment.

So in this obsession, when the leader notices other people who might have the ability to be his successors, he perceives them as threats to his power. This perception can even lead the leader to develop arrogant behaviours which show others around him that, "I am invincible at this leadership title".

In this view, the leader can end up lacking the qualities to lead ethically, as he may develop behaviours that may hurt people. Thus, this type of leadership can take down the Eagle from its glory honoured perspective into an enemy of the people, or business which he might have sworn to protect.

Signs which shows need to step down as a leader

➢ when you no longer produce new ideas

➢ when there is someone better waiting in the wings

➢ when developing enmity with more important relationships

➢ when employee turnover has become too common

➢ when stress is killing you

If the leader does not have someone who he believes to be his successor, he has to groom one who has to be more effective than him. This strategy can give a sense of comfort for the leader to leave gracefully while leaving his name respected and honoured for his humility. So, humility builds greatness in a leader by developing awareness around his limitations, and willingness to overcome forces that leads to power obsession. (…will further discuss humility in the next chapter)

A typical leader who refused to step down

Case study

Robert Mugabe got in office on 31 December 1987 as president of Zimbabwe, which he was preceded by Canaan Banana who ruled from 18 April 1980 to 1987. He pursued decolonisation and emphasised the land redistribution of land controlled by white farmers to blacks who didn't own much land. He first did this through 'willing buyer- willing seller', and however got frustrated by how slow the rate of distribution was. From 2000 he then encouraged black Zimbabweans to violently seize white-owned farms. After then, food production was severely impacted, leading to famine, economic decline, and western sanctions. This economical downfall led Mugabe's opposition to grew, but he was re-elected into power in 2002, 2008, and 2013, through campaigns that were dominated by violence and controversial electoral frauds. After being in power for 37 years, on 21 November 2017 members of his party after noticing his power obsession, forced him out replacing him with president Emerson Mnangagwa.

Apart from being obsessed with power, Robert Mugabe was praised as a revolutionary hero of the African liberation struggle who helped to free Zimbabwe from British colonialism, imperialism, and the white minority rule. Long live the king!

However, he had his limitations which on them should have groomed a successor to fight economic mismanagement, human rights abuses, anti-white racism, corruption, and crimes against humanity. So, for the leader to avoid this fall, one must be aware of when to step down and allow other individuals who possess leadership qualities to help build greatness.

Chapter 6

THE LION: "as a man think in his mind, so is he"- biblical wisdom

The Great Leader

This is an individual who possesses extended humility and professional will to build enduring greatness through consistent self-control.

Beliefs of the Lion

A great leader believes that the reality of life is made within an individual's mind, meaning the beliefs one possesses towards something, creates an individual's reality. In this psychology, there is no crisis to an individual, and everything is an opportunity to do something valuable. This interpretation then develops a ready-to embrace awareness towards those presented opportunities even if they might seem unfavourable for an individual. As an individual grows to interpret everything as an opportunity in life, he then organises and prepares himself and the surrounding team to take chances for success. In this awareness the lion also believes that no one in his environment can determine what he can do and or what he cannot do, believing he is in charge of his own life and destiny.

This mindset is also strengthened by the belief that God already gave humans the ability to be great leaders from his greatness in

(Genesis 1:26) when God created a human being in his image, likeliness, and gave him the power to rule all other living creatures and earth resources. In this belief, an individual grows to be aware that I was given the authority and capabilities of a leader by God. Thus, a great leader desire to own these resources, powers, and rule as per creation by creator God, and when other individuals don't possess these resources yet, or not believing in their powers to own these resources but desire them, he employs. In this awareness, greatness then comes when an individual grooms other individuals who also believe in growing into great leaders, by teaching them how to become one.

Through these lion beliefs, an individual can see the importance and potential of everyone in life and around work. The great leader believes that everyone is a leader in the area they operate in regardless of what position they work at. However many people do not think that they are meant to lead and denied the fact that everyone is a leader by saying "if everyone is a leader, who will follow"? Thus, this belief shows that society has successfully convinced them out of their true self by injecting viruses into their heads in form of doubt and fear.

An individual with the Lion belief understands that people get power to do something through their belief systems, for example, Lion's mentality can make an average person believe that he is a leader, and can hire someone who has reached top-notch in schooling to manage his business towards greatness. In this mindset, an individual is aware that, he does not need to be educated that much in-order to hire someone who is, in his business. Through these beliefs, Lion's attitude reduces other educated individuals into workers, meaning that when an individual possesses this belief, he will see other individuals with high rated skills, who might not know what to do with those skills as employees.

So, in this mentality, an individual knows that he is demanded to improve more frequently in mentality than skills since leadership is 80% percent psychology and only 20% skill. Being also aware that no matter how many skills an individual possesses, if that individual does not have the attitude ignited by a great leader's belief, he will work for those who have.

Desires and Values

Great leaders desire human transformation by showing other individuals their capabilities which lie beyond the other side of fear and knowledge. They desire to do this since it's in their ability to turn frightened people into fearless individuals through their words and motivations. They can provide guidance and wisdom to those who seek it, then shows them ways on how to become even greater leaders.

In this mindset, the Lion desires to create a very strong team of few but truly committed and skilled people around. An individual desires to create a strong team in these values because he knows that for someone to grow from nothing into success then greatness, he needs help from other individuals who have strong vision and skills. This desire in an individual to surround oneself with skilled and committed individuals leads a being to have fewer friends, leaving other individuals and environments which do not help in stepping further into greatness. Chosen positive environments and talented beings around the leader are picked based on purpose. Helping the leader to shut doors for all toxic influences which might drain the energy of growth and development, creating a discipline from within and around which set some boundaries and values.

Spiritual perceptions

Purpose-driven

(Proverbs19:21)...Many are plans in a person's heart, but it is the lord's purpose that prevails

In this perception, an individual is aware that when a manufacturer(God) makes a product(Human), he makes it perform specific functions and builds into the product, the capacity to perform the function. Thus, if a being wants to know the purpose of the product(himself), he does not ask the product to tell him, but rather he goes to the manufacturer to ask how it works. In this perception, the individual understands that "only God knows how I operate and if anyone tells me otherwise it's a red flag of a virus to get rid of, out of my mind".

Simply, to accomplish connections with the manufacturer or creator God an individual with this perception pray, meditate and work towards desires in life.

Bible scriptures on purpose

God has a purpose for everyone

(Exodus 9:16)...but I have raised you for this purpose, that I might show you my power and that my name might be proclaimed in all the earth.

God's purpose cannot be undone

(Job 42:2)...I know you can do all things, no purpose of yours can be thwarted

God's purpose is the one that lasts

(Proverbs 19:21)...many are plans in a person's heart, but it is the lord's purpose that prevails.

Passion driven

(Psalm 37:4-5).."Take delight in the lord, and he will give you the desires of your heart.

In this perception, the lion is very determined to get what he wants, with emphasis on being stubborn. His determination and stubbornness help him to reach greater heights in business and personal life, if he is not that committed, the dream would be easy to give up. Thus, for an individual with this behaviour to succeed, he has to set goals, putting all available resources together and individual efforts to accomplish desired goals.

In this drive, to avoid chasing desires blindly, an individual has to be clear to oneself when looking at a life situation, to determine if he is chasing his real passion or just hot passion of the day (chasing something because a lot of people are making it through that particular thing today).

Being clear to oneself helps an individual's spirituality to stay growing by looking into the future while being prepared to come up with the best decisions in those situations. This requires an individual to look back at life for a clear picture of how he wanted the future to be like right now, aligning new and old choices with individual skills.

So in this perception, being passion-driven makes an individual tirelessly work around gifts and talents, to embrace new opportunities in the goal chasing journey.

Life has ups and has downs

(2 chronicles 15:7) ..."But as for you, be strong and do not give up, for your work will be rewarded".

This spiritual perception makes the leader very flexible and relentless towards life when working to achieve desired goals. In this perception, an individual sets goals and plans towards achieving, bearing in mind that anything can happen in this journey. This awareness helps to know when to become which as the situations may change, demanding to also change into adaptation to build businesses and personalities into greatness.

Note, the great leader does not retreat when confronted by setbacks and uncertainties, he pushes forward with help of his master-mind team to lean forward into the future by making up the best ideas, which may get the next best possible outcomes. In this perception, an individual is aware that life is never a straight path, so when life throws a punch to him in form of losses, he is ready to take a punch and continue his business with modified future approaches.

Understanding this spirituality can lead an individual to develop an unwavering vision without fear of the uncertainty in life's ups and downs. This awareness grows an individual spirituality in form of patience around others and oneself during those ups and downs. However, If an individual fails with this awareness, should be able to embrace failure which occurred due to past actions, and take it as a lesson to grow spiritually by understanding that every failed experiment brings one step closer to achieving a dream.

Educational perceptions

Extending knowledge

The lion understands that knowledge-seeking is an endless process that should be updated constantly for an individual to stay on top of whatever he does. The great leader continues learning till becoming the domain expect of his inventions and continues extending personal knowledge to avoid getting trapped by that knowledge.

An individual can extend knowledge by always keeping up a beginner's mind which helps to glance at situations freshly from the past know-how. Thus, in this awareness an individual can see, what he knows, and what he does not know, creating extended awareness around an individual's weaknesses and strengths.

In this perception, the lion being is willing to learn how to make personal weaknesses average by developing basic understandings, while also extending existing knowledge and skills to build greatness.

When an individual seeks knowledge extension, personal vision and perceptions are also improved further through exploring different cultures, economies, and places.

Personal experiences can grow a great leader into understanding why people in different environments think differently, and behave differently.

When an individual understands why different people behave the way they do, he can even know how to associate with them and approach them with new ideas which can change their lives and perceptions, - building business ethically.

Questioning information

A great leader is presented with various information from different people's opinions and judgements on him and the future. In this perception, an individual should listen to other people but weighing the stimuli of their words. So, if people are giving opinions due to fear and limitations of their minds, the leader should acknowledge them but goes back into his personal gallery to seek motivation from past successes similar or worse to the presented situations.

In this perception, an individual does not like information which reduces the way he thinks of himself since he knows his intentions, willing to do whatever it takes to achieve desired dream goal. He understands that some of the information is spread to make people weak and steal the leadership out of them, making them believe in greater forces beyond their control.

So, when an individual with this perception come across negative influences, he has a way to prevent attending to the stimuli and also going back to rehearse what made him think the way he did after being exposed to the virus of negativity

Let's take for instance, if an individual with this perception walks into society and tries to tell people that, "we are all leaders", what do you think happens?

People will point to him as a mad man or someone who doesn't understand that leading is meant for other people not everyone. This belief was brought to each one of them as they grew in the society, and when individuals with this perception seek information to improve their lives, they don't touch the aspect of leadership since they accepted that it's not theirs. This happens to every child being born in that society (virus) even if the parent thinks otherwise because **'it takes a village to raise a child'**. So, everyone in society has a role they play in influencing the mindset of every other individual they encounter, even if you don't notice, you do.

These influences make the great perceiver aware, and question information whenever it is represented to him. Asking questions to see if he can attend to the presented information or not by evaluating the importance of that information in life, asking questions like, How can 1 use this? Why must 1 use this ?, and When can 1 use this? In these attentive evaluations, an individual can find out how to use the presented information,- and if it is relevant to the purpose.

Note, these attending questions also help even if the individual is learning new information, making it stuck in the mind by creating interesting emotions which boost the individual's attention.

Financial Perceptions

Generational wealth

Individuals who desire wealth, create finances that grow into passive financial returns in the future. In this perception, an individual understands the importance of working now, to achieve those financial returns.

When money grows into generational wealth, it can cover up for even future individual expenses, while placing an individual in a ready to invest position towards new sound business opportunities. However, business opportunities require the individual to possess some skills and knowledge which enables to read the market's future trend. This then helps the individual to make wise investment choices, while influencing other people to help in the appreciation of the investment value through social media and interview appearances, and such.

As the individual grows to become a great financial leader, it will be easy to find more investments since the background, reputation might be convincing to lenders and business partners to work with them. However, possession of wealth in abundance can lead the individual to dominate financially, developing monopolies around businesses, or other unethical behaviours which might hurt other less fortunate individuals.

So, an individual with desire should be aware that, this desire has to develop willingness within to maintain personal humility and self-control, also allowing other individuals to grow their dreams.

Who is owing who?

The great financial leader's perceptions develop awareness within an individual around this question (who is owing who), understanding that, 'if people don't owe me money, it means I owe them money.'

When an individual makes a business deal with this perception, he tries to reduce the number of people to whom he owes while increasing the number of people who owe him. The individual master this by understanding that, 'when you owe people money, it means you are indebted to them, and money is flowing from you to them, and on the other hand …if people owe you money, it means that money is now flowing from them to you'….now its good for business right?

A great financial leader is also aware that, 'who is owing who?' process begins the moment an individual takes the other individual's hand financially for help around business or personal interests. Thus, in this psychology, what differentiates a financial great leader from other individuals is that if he owes someone or another party money, he understands that money will be flowing from him, and it is demanded from him the ability to see a way through which cover that debt with the acquired asset or other investments.

Simply, the debt should give you more money than you owed.

Paying low to no taxes

When one becomes an investor chances of paying taxes is slim than an ordinary worker and small business. For example, if the individual owns a large company, the government will charge high taxes on the workers and very low taxes on the business corporation.

In business, the lion perceiver makes sure that he does not put anything in his name around business, instead forms a company as a separate legal entity. So, the owner's involvement in the business will be noticed as an employee of the company, making the owner's tax charges dissociated with possession of the company.

In this perception, business major tax benefits to the government will come when it charges high taxes on employees while relieving the company from paying high taxes. So, no need to make the owner vultures meat, why?

The Lion being is aware that, the government does not charge high taxes on large corporations since it perceives that, 'if the business gets extra profit with room to acquire more assets, it will hire more employees to increase productivity, and in this process, as the business employs more workers, the government benefits by charging taxes on the company's new and existing employees'.

So, in this perception, the owner's business is not affected, and will be determined to hire more employees who will increase returns as profits, while a large percentage of tax charges fall on them (employees).....

············

The great leader personality

Extended Humility

A great leader is a truthful being who is very honest about personal intentions in life and business.

In this personality, an individual says things that have to be said and if people try to hide the truth, he makes it open for everyone to understand, with emphasis on being transparent. However, in this personality, the individual does not do things to please crowds but rather being true to oneself while attracting the right people around. So, the great leader appreciates few people around, who are truly committed to helping in the achievement of the goal.

This personality also helps the leader to be a great motivator around other people who works with him, in achieving their own desired dreams and business objectives. The great leader does this by teaching other individuals how to become leaders in business and personal life through shared perceptions and experiences.

If employees or followers grow the abilities to lead, the great leader connects them to new opportunities in life enhancing their chances of becoming other great leaders. Thus, in this personality, the great leader has it in mind that, 'people who work for him one day will leave and lead in other organisations.

With this awareness, the leader grows by trying to give other people's lives meaning in an organisation and society. Doing this with the understanding that, 'the individual's life begins when one perceives its meaning'.

In this awareness, the other individual will grow to know what he is supposed to attend to while aligning every action with the desired goal. For example, when an individual with Lion's personality come across someone who desires to be a businessman in life, he shows the other individual how to understand the desired journey, and what it takes to be a winner in that journey by knowing which type of books to read, type of news to seek, type of mentors to follow, thus, every stimulus has to push the individual towards purpose.

Furthermore, the humility of a great leader grows individual self-awareness, the awareness which helps to understand more of individual capabilities and limitations. In this personality, when the individual grows humility while knowing personal limitations, it grows the willingness to account for other individuals' contributions which might help to bring the goal closer, reducing costs in the way.

So, humility creates room for strong listening skills which weigh the information that is already on the table with other added opinions and facts, making it possible for the humble leader to admit his own bias and correct if there is any.

Professional will

Great leaders are people who don't seek titles in life, but rather are servants of their desires. When engaging in professional activities, they show strong leadership skills through determination and dedication to the team.

They also seek deeper perceptions around the value of others and their add towards the success of an organisation, growing willingness within to groom other individuals with the potential to be better leaders.

In this personality, the great leader is willing to give the groomed a chance to be improved by showing limitations to his past successes, and ways on how to overcome these limitations in the future.

Professional will grow a leader to allow other capable individuals to take charge, doing what he does when unavailable, preparing others to be independent thinkers when they lead on their own. However, as the leader grooms other leaders, he should be there to guide them with wisdom and knowledge, while testing their authenticity.

Thus, when the leader possesses extended humility and professional will to build enduring greatness through consistent self-control, he can build a company, church, and or a political party that can survive for many years.

Shaping others behaviours

The great leader shows people who work around him personal intentions, and business expectations to every team member. In this personality, the leader is willing to show other people what it takes to be in a particular position through words and actions.

When a leader with this personality says something, he shows integrity by acting, so that others may follow. This personality helps the leader to communicate his intentions, to grow expected behaviours in others at work.

How a great leader shapes behaviours

✓ by words

✓ by actions

✓ by his behaviour

✓   And by connecting with followers

Thus, If an individual is not willing to feed through the discipline, the great leader is willing to lose that person from the team, being aware that the individual's presence will cause distractions to him and others in achieving business goals.

Overcoming oppositions

Oppositions exist around the leader's world and when they do, an individual with a lion personality does not catch feelings, which may create enmity with the opposing forces.

This personality as an individual does not create unnecessary enemies due to emotional stimuli. If other people tell him 'you are wrong' or oppose, he may try to understand by asking 'in what way? after growing the awareness, the leader acknowledges oppositions, not taking anything personally, while developing courage within to make valuable relationships work.

However, if the oppositions are very determined to take the leader down, in this personality the leader should seek enough understanding about their ground and desires, predicting their next moves which may be used against him, also measuring the consequences of those actions.

Growing this awareness, lead the leader to calculate any damage if oppositions grow against him, and can seek to make the first move in getting rid of the enemies gracefully.

Enemies are given room to leave gracefully in business and around personal life to avoid more controversies, vengeance and terminated cooperation which might deter the leader's important life goals.

For example at work, a leader can avoid unnecessary opposition by avoiding unexpected firing and retrenchment of employees which is against the law, causing more dramas with the labour unions. So if the leader wishes to let someone go due to many causes which might slow down goal achievement, he should be open when communicating with the individual.

Thus in this scenario, a great leader may give the leaving individual benefiting compensations which can help to survive the unemployed for some time, while providing links to other companies, making the individual leave in peace.

Bonus: Anger and intolerance

Great leaders don't tolerate nonsense, when people break boundaries they can get angry! showing a lack of interest around undesired actions. In this personality, an individual can get angry or irritated by situations that can be controlled but heading wood. Thus, when the leader notices something undesirable, he does not go silent but instead says it is enough, then moves to a more productive option. This inability to tolerate everything makes a leader an agent of change. However, trying to grow tolerance around undesired situations can lead a leader into doom. As the saying goes," *toleration is the graveyard of leaders"*, since whatever the leader tolerates he does not change.

··········

Perception stimuli

An individual with the lion psychology was once a follower, and or a worker who was mentored to think differently corresponding to his self-discovery. Once perceiving himself as a sheep, but something happened which made him discover his abilities that grew into Lion's psychology.

When growing up the individual discovered that it takes steps to grow one's perceptions to match that of a leader. Thus, for an individual to be a leader, he should start within by seeing everything from a leader's perspective.

This understanding gave the leader awareness about how different people solve life situations differently, depending on individual's life perceptions.

In this awareness, a leader grew to cancel all excuses of not becoming a leader and discovered that for an individual to be a leader, he does not need to be the most intelligent or talented but rather having the mentality of a lion which views situations on a leader's perspective. For example in the wild, a tiger is 16% more intelligent than a lion, and elephants are the strongest and so many other animals with extended abilities, but in the lion's mind, they are all lunch, believing that nothing can take him down.

So, resembling an individual with the lion mindset around business and life, this being does not get threatened by how educated, skilled and talented others are, but rather see a way to benefit and improve oneself.

Note, an individual with Lion's psychology has to discover the connection between the creator God and a human being since it is the true introduction to oneself. With this awareness, an individual can learn how to follow the steps of the creator God, by first believing to have creative abilities as the creator God's image.

....

The difference:

(The Lion vs The Tiger)-(Great leader vs Own boss)

Both individuals who possess the lion or the tiger resemblance want to be owners and rulers. They all want to control resources independently and are ready for the next big challenges that are presented for the growth of their personality and business careers. However, when the tiger starts a business, he needs to be present for that business to survive. The tiger performs everything crucial in business by himself, and if he is not present at work, nothing will be productive. Thus, the tiger's time is demanded to keep the business running. The tiger's behaviour of running a business solo is stimulated by the way he views business, perceiving that other people cannot be trusted to perform his duties since they are not like him. Thus, delegating in this perception is risky since it can lead the business to lose clients...(in his head of course).

An individual with the lion's psychology, on the other hand, can run a business even in absence for a long period, coming back to see the business more productive than it was before. He trains and provides resources to the team, developing other individual's skills and knowledge on how to run successfully those resources.

In this psychology, as the business grows bigger, the individual is relieved from his duties and can start other businesses, also having other time on vacations with family and business research. Thus, an individual with the lion's perceptions can see the importance of delegating business tasks to other capable and skilled individuals.

The tiger being is smarter, knowing what to provide customers with to get a financial return. Thus, performing business research to understand what people want, and then provide the right product or services at unique quality.

The Lion being hires experts in a particular area, for example, sales management, accounting management, research and other departments to perform business operations in return for compensations and opportunities. These skilled individuals then help the business in growing the market, finances, product features, and business management as a whole. However, in this psychology, a leader should possess awareness around the general flowing of each department's business activity, to determine independently which direction to go.

If an individual with the tiger's psychology is convinced to outsource some of the business tasks, without growing individual leadership perceptions, he can push employees to work towards objectives like a manager. Thus, a managing Tiger can push workers to perform like him, ending up being disappointed or frustrated when those workers fail to see the world or situations similarly.

On the other hand, a great leader seeks the right people in his team. Making sure that the selected individuals do not need to be pushed to greater heights but rather push themselves. However, it is perceived that in business, hiring is guessing- meaning the leader can sometimes hire the wrong individuals. Thus after finding out, unlike the Tiger being who pushes workers to become what they don't want to be, the leader gives the other individual graceful exist from the team, communicating why's around that decision.

Simply!. The tiger being thinks that no one can do what he does best in life and business, while the Lion being understands that he does not need to be the best at everything but to become a leader who hires people with the right character, knowledge, and talents in the business.

Chapter 7

Conclusion

Operating on different faces: when to become who?

As I grew into understanding, I realised that in the leadership journey, you can graduate from all the stated staircases, developing eagerness to want to possess the power of the leader in an instant. That's the goal, but as you grew up to this stage, you might personally don't possess the resources to lead an organisation but you surely can attract these resources now.

> Whether you want to lead or guide a group of people towards the accomplishment of an objective, you are demanded more patience, persistence, transparency, humbleness, and seeking more knowledge to build these resources from scratch or continual growth of the established.

I advise reading the book on repeat and or taking the qualities you want to grow on a written note, in this written note you can create goals to see if you are following up with what you have learned for it to become you. As the common saying similarly states, "if you learn something and fail to apply the knowledge, you are not much of a difference from an illiterate person".

So, for continuous growth, an individual needs to understand that he/she does not know everything, so there is a need to follow, while other times leading, depending on the possessed knowledge, skills, and experience on a particular subject.

Since now you know what it takes to handle yourself like a great leader, lead others in a humble way. With this, it is most likely that what you build will last into greatness.

So in with awareness, you have to know when to work like the OX?, when to manage like the Elephant?, when to do things smarter like the Tiger? and when to develop a vision for the future like the eagle?.

Reminder!. don't forget to help others in reaching their own goals.

In this journey, you earned the necessary knowledge to interpret a presented environment like a greater leader, it's now up to you to choose a path you want to lead your life into. As stated earlier, this book is not strictly meant for people who want to build organisations but also to help others rebuild their own life by believing in themselves, creating their desires, being aware of the demanded qualities to build personalities that can last from the ground.

Best regards.

Bibliography

Bandura, Albert and Walters, Richard H. (1963). Social Learning and Personality Development. New York. Holt, Rinehart & Winston.

Bass, B. M. (n.d.). From transactional to transformational leadership: Learning to share the vision. Organizational Dynamics 19-31.

Braham, B. J. (1995). Creating A Learning Organization. Menlo Park, CA: Crisp Publications, Inc.

Blackwell Encyclopedic Dictionary of Human Resource Management. (1997). Malden, Massachusetts. Blackwell Publishers.

Covey, Stephen R. The 7 Habits of Highly Effective People Personal Workbook. New York: Simon & Schuster, 2003.

Dean Graziosi. Millionaire Success habits, 2017

Duquette, D. J., & Stowe, A. M. (1992). Financial management in the public sector. The Government Accountants Journal, XLI(2), 18-28.

Elizabeth J. Akers, Matthew M. Chingos December 2017, Are college students borrowing blindly?

Gates, Lisa R., and Hellweg, Susan A. (1989). The Socializing Function of New Employee Orientation Programs: A Study of Organizational Identification and Job Satisfaction. Paper presented at the Annual Meeting of the Western Speech Communication Association. Spokane, WA. February 17-21, 1989.

Gronn, Peter. 1995. "Greatness Revisited: The Current Obsession with Transformational Leadership." Leading and Managing 1:14–27 (http://staff.edfac.unimelb .edu.au/david_gurr/482–707/gronn_95.html).

Genius Steve Jobs vs Bill Gates, history TV

Goleman, Daniel, et.al. Primal Leadership: Learning to Lead with Emotional Intelligence. Boston: Harvard Business School Press. 2002.

Jacob's story, In the Jewish bible, in Genesis 29

Jeffrey Pfeffer & Associates, Power, Why Some People Have It, And Others Don't,2010

Jim Collins & Associates, Good To Great, Why Some Companies Make The Leap, And Others Don't,2001

Kapoor, J.R., Dlabay, L.R., Hughes, R.J., & Hart, M.M. (2016). Focus on Personal Finance. New York,
NY: McGraw Hill Education.

Kotter, John. 1996. Leading Change. Boston: Harvard Business School Press.

Kouzes, James M.; Posner, Barry Z. Encouraging the Heart: A Leader's Guide to Rewarding and Recognizing Others. The Jossey-Bass Business & Management Series.211p, 1999

Labovitz, G., Rosansky, V., & Varian, T. (1994). Leadership: Taking charge of change. Burlington, MA: Organizational Dynamics, Inc.

Latham, J. R. (1995, April). Visioning: The concept, trilogy, and process. Quality Progress, 65-68.

Locke, E. The Essence of Leadership: Four Keys to Leading Successfully. San Francisco CA: New Lexington Press, 1991.

Managing for results: Critical actions for measuring performance: Testimony before the Subcommittee on Government Management, Information, and Technology, Committee on Government Reform and Oversight, House of Representatives. (GAO Publication No. GAO/T-GGD/AIMD-95-187). (1995). Testimony of J. C. Finch & C. Hoenig. Washington, DC: United States General Accounting

Maxwell, John C. The 5 Levels of Leadership. New York: Center Street. 2011.

Metz, E. (1984). Managing change: Implementing productivity and quality improvements. National Productivity Review, 3(3), 303-314.

Paine, L. S. (1994, March-April). Managing for organizational integrity. Harvard Business Review, 106-117.

Research. Cited in Greenberg, J. 2011. Behaviour in Organisations (10

Edition). Pearson.

Robbins, S., Judge, T. and Campbell, T. 2010. Organizational Behaviour. Harlow: Pearson. Rowe

Robert Kiyosaki & Associates Cash Flow Quadrant, Guide To Financial Freedom, 2015

Schein, E. H. (1990, February). Organizational culture. American Psychologist, 109-119.

Senge, Peter. "The Leader's New Work: Building Learning Organizations," Sloan Management Review, V32N1, (Fall 1990): 7-23.

Senge, P. M., Roberts, C., Ross, R. B., Smith, B. J., & Kleiner, A. (1994). The Fifth Discipline Fieldbook. New York: Doubleday.

Should You Ever Prepay Your Mortgage? (2014). Daily Worth: https://www.dailyworth.com/posts/2359-should-you-prepay-your-mortgage. The High Cost of Credit Card Minimum Payments (2015). extension: http://articles.extension.org/pages/25259/the-high-cost-of-credit-card-minimum-payments.

Sink, D. S. (1985, January). Strategic planning: A crucial step toward a successful productivity management program. IE, 52-60.

The Collapse of Lehman Brothers: A Case Study.By NICK LIOUDIS, Reviewed by MARGARET JAMES.2021

'The Fatherhood of God in Christian Truth and Life. By J. SCOTT LIDGETT, M.A.
New York: Imported by Scribner.

Robert Mugabe, Wikipedia

The Psychology of Prayer: A Scientific Approach. By Bernard Spilka and Kevin L. Ladd.

The Richest Man in Babylon by George S. Clason, 1926

Thompson, A., Strickland, A. and Gamble, J. 2007. Corporate Culture and Leadership. Crafting and Executing Strategy: Concepts and Cases (15th

Edition). McGraw Hill.

Tichy, N.M. The Leadership Engine: How Winning Companies Build Leaders at Every Level. New York: HarperBusiness, 1997.

Treacy, M., & Wiersema, F. (1995). The Discipline of Market Leaders. Reading, MA: Addison-Wesley Publishing.

Understanding Credit Card Interest (2016). Investopedia: http://www.investopedia.com/articles/01/061301.asp.

ABOUT THE AUTHOR

Tatenda D Nduru is a business management and entrepreneurship student at the Chinhoyi University Of Technology in Zimbabwe, who grew most of his knowledge through self-education to understand his desire to be a great leader, to build fortune, relationships and personality which last in legends.